FAITH IN DARK PLACES

David Rhodes is an Anglican priest based in the multi-racial inner city parish of Chapeltown in Leeds. He works part-time with the ecumenical Faith in Leeds project helping suburban Christians to engage with inner city social justice issues such as homelessness. He also works as a volunteer with homeless and alcoholic people and runs city centre 'retreats on the streets'.

In 1989 he started the Prayer Light candle meditations to help people in his own church to pray. Since then it has become a nationwide ministry.

He is a former national newspaper journalist and has done extensive communications work for the Church Urban Fund which he says is the best thing the Church of England has set up in the last fifty years.

FAITH IN DARK PLACES

David Rhodes

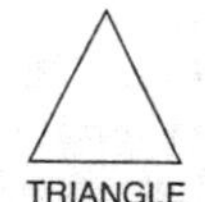

First published in Great Britain in 1996
Triangle
SPCK
Holy Trinity Church
Marylebone Road
London NW1 4DU

NOTE
All royalties from the sale of this book are going directly to the Church Urban Fund.

ACKNOWLEDGEMENTS
Unless otherwise stated, biblical quotations are from *The New English Bible* (NEB) copyright © 1961, 1970 Oxford and Cambridge University Presses.
Extracts from the *Revised Standard Version* (RSV) are copyright © 1971 and 1952.
Psalm 143 (p. 56) is slightly amended from the Authorized Version of the Bible, the text of which is the property of the Crown in perpetuity.

British Library Cataloguing-in-Publication Data
A catalogue record of this book is available from the British Library

ISBN 0–281–04986–6

Typeset by Wilmaset Ltd, Birkenhead, Wirral
Printed in Great Britain by
BPC Paperbacks Ltd.

CONTENTS

FOREWORD

Every so often, by the grace of God (and I mean this literally), a writer or preacher is given the gift of opening up the scriptures for some of his fellow men and women. David Rhodes is such a writer. His book reminds me of Andrew Greeley's *The Sinai Myth* which brought the book of Exodus to life for me.

What Greeley did for me is to explain that the Sinai event, that wild theophany of thunder and lightning, was revealing to the people of Israel, and eventually to us, that El Shaddai, the God of Sinai, was not only all-powerful but also all-loving. Surprise, surprise, Yahweh, the God of the Mountain, of wind and storm, loves his people with a love beyond their wildest dreams. It was Yahweh God who rescued his beloved people from slavery, who carried them in the desert, as a father carries his child, who pursued them when they rebelled, chasing after them as a man pursues his unfaithful wife, cornering them as a shepherd catches the last exhausted runaway lamb.

It is hard to explain just how life-giving this discovery was for me, how it gave me an anchor of hope in a rough and changing world. Bishops and popes come and go, my devotional life varies with the seasons of my heart, but rain or shine, I know, like the Israelites of old, that the God who made the universe is also the God of my hearth, the God to whom I can talk.

David Rhodes' book is about this same God, incarnate in Jesus of Nazareth, and it has spoken to me with the same powerful clarity. After years of struggling to feel an affinity with the 'gentle Jesus, meek and mild' of my childhood, it is as though the optician has suddenly slipped the correct lens into my spectacles so that I exclaim 'That's it, now I can see!' What speaks to me is the description of Jesus drawn from a study of the parables: 'an often passionately angry young man' whose dynamic teaching had political implications. This comment reminds me of the monk Tom Cullinan's remark that we were given a gospel which is a wild stallion but we have domesticated it into a riding school pony.

David Rhodes is intent upon rediscovering the wild stallion in the gospel: the way in which Jesus threatens the status quo of a domesticated, complacent religious establishment by reminding it of the nature and will of the God it purports to worship. The passionate young man, the 'Christ-person', he describes is infinitely more attractive than the long-haired wimp of pious lithograph. His Jesus has more in common (dare I say it) with Bob Geldof when he was campaigning for the starving people of Africa. 'Give us yer money!' he shouted, exasperated. 'If you mess about any longer, these people will die of hunger. Do you hear me? They'll die!'

I don't know how to swear in Aramaic, but I'll bet you Jesus did, and if that suggestion shocks you, think again. If Jesus was a man like us in all things but sin, if he was friendly with social outcasts and prostitutes, had rows with the religious establishment of the day and was eventually killed because he was a threat to the status quo, is it reasonable to imagine him as a quietly-spoken, polite young man? My guess is that he was more like some of my missionary friends who weep and swear in fury over the plight of the poor whom they serve: the poor whose babies die of malnutrition and now of AIDS. Jesus is the incarnation, the enfleshing, of the real God of the Old Testament, the God of Sinai, the God of the *anawim*, the marginalized, the under-dog.

ACKNOWLEDGEMENTS

I would like to thank some very special people whose lives have been an inspiration to me, although in the eyes of the world they may not seem very important. They are people like Mick and Brian, Corinne, Jack and Lee.

Material for the 'bible study' sections of this book has been drawn from a variety of sources: some half-remembered – others forgotten. Inspiration, and confirmation of my own ideas has come from William Barclay, *The Gospel of Mark* and *The Gospel of Luke* (St Andrew Press 1975); Ed Kessler on conflict in the parables in *The Good Samaritan* (Sheffield Urban Theology Unit 1992); D. E. Nineham, *Saint Mark* (Pelican New Testament Commentaries 1963); John J. Vincent and John D. Davies, *Mark at Work* (Bible Reading Fellowship 1986). Peter Ball, formerly Bishop of Gloucester (heard on an amateur recording at a conference), is acknowledged with gratitude.

None has been knowingly quoted: all have been greatly appreciated.

1
The Big Question

THIS BOOK IS an ordinary person's attempt to answer a very important question. The question is simply: what is real in this life?

Each of us might want to ask the question in a slightly different way: what is there in this life that means anything? What is there that matters? What does it mean to be alive? And does it mean anything?

Seeking after 'reality' may sound as pointless as chasing after shadows, but perhaps we will find that when we actually engage in that search we shall make a surprising discovery.

The book explores the unlikely suggestion that much of what western society counts important is probably a huge deception: but that unexpectedly, those things and those people we often dismiss as being worthless may in fact be the most real and precious.

It is a story about failure and about hope. Its heroes are people whom society despises for being unemployed, homeless, and sometimes alcoholic. People counted as worthless; but who in strange and fragmentary ways, and despite their human weakness, faults and confusions, seem to embody what is real. People materially so poor and physically so ill who can yet show us things of immense value; people who live close to death but who reveal to us what it means to be alive.

This book is not about religion but it is about God. It is about people and pain; failure and courage; laughter and prayer.

Who is it for? It is for people uneasy with the prevailing values of western society; people on the fringes of the Church; people who may suspect their own lives to be hollow; who want to find a worth which does not damage or exploit others.

People who want to be able to make sense of life; and to be allowed, in their own space and time, to encounter God. It may even be for the Church as it seeks a deeper encounter with God and struggles to respond to that meeting.

And who is it from? It is from people consigned to the margins of society from where, it is assumed, they have nothing and can give nothing. People who may be the very ones who can give us life.

How it Began

This story was not planned: it was discovered, almost by accident. It was stumbled upon by people intent on doing other things, who gradually realized that the world is not entirely as they thought it was, and that the voice of God may be heard in the most unlikely places.

They are people like the man taking part in a church project to learn about life in the deprived areas of the inner city.

The catch was that the people taking part in the project were not going to learn by reading books – they were going to learn by doing: walking the streets and meeting the people.

Above all, they would be following the pattern of Christ, who challenged his disciples with the words: 'follow me.' Come from where you are and where you feel safe, to where I am. It sounded easy, but for many people this was a demanding and uncomfortable experience as one participant discovered:

SAME CITY: DIFFERENT WORLD

As he parked the car the man was angry. He was angry with himself. Switching off the car engine he sat for a long time as if unsure what to do next. He looked at the slip of paper with the hand-drawn street map on it.

Reluctantly, he got out of the car and looked uneasily around him. The car was new and glistened in the sun; the street was old and shabby as is much of that part of the inner city. The car's automatic locking and alarm system sounded piercingly loud and the man glanced anxiously around.

He realized that the car stood out in the poverty of the surrounding area. Even his clothes, some faded jeans and an old golfing sweater, looked out of place. He was just three miles away from his own home in the leafy suburbs. It was the same city but it might as well have been a different planet. He was a stranger here.

The man was angry because he was afraid. He was in one of the worst areas of the city for muggings. This was well known. He had often read in the papers about people being knifed by young thugs wanting money for drugs. This was a place of danger and he felt vulnerable and very much alone. He glanced at his little map again and set off. He had been given a task and it was too late to turn back.

His task was an important one: to pray.

Along with twenty other people, who were also to set out alone to walk these unfamiliar streets of the inner city, he had been asked to spend the next half-hour in prayer.

He was setting out on a walking meditation. This idea is well known in religious retreats, where people walk country lanes and reflect on the blessings of God's creation. In the quietness of their walk they become aware of colours, textures, scents and sounds: the blue of the sky, the sound of birdsong, and the wind in the trees. It is a way of praying using the world around them instead of familiar religious words.

Walking meditations are familiar in retreat work: but not in the multi-racial inner city with its broken pavements and boarded-up shops; where trees are things for kids to swing on and few birds sing.

As the man walked down the street he felt uneasy; and unsure whether he would return unharmed. And would his car still be there if he did? He scanned the pavement ahead for signs of danger and found himself listening for running feet behind him as a mugger closed in. But there were only two women with a pram. They broke off their conversation to smile and say good morning. And the only footsteps he could hear were his own.

Gradually, as he walked, the fear began to recede and the world came back into focus. He turned into a busy street and was suddenly hit by the din of traffic as buses, cars and heavy commercial vehicles choked the air with exhaust fumes. A few yards away in cramped side streets people lived in the most densely populated area of northern Europe.

The man thought of his own home with its lawns, the new conservatory, and the double garage. He thought of his own children with their school uniforms and music lessons. Children whose lives were a million miles from here.

Occasionally he remembered he was supposed to be praying. He wondered what God was making of all this mess. And what the answer was.

Finally, still clutching his crumpled map, the man completed the long circular route. He had not been mugged, and ahead down the street he could see his car. Amazingly, it had not been stolen or vandalized.

The people he had encountered had been friendly. He thought back to the greengrocer's where he had bought a lettuce. Why a lettuce? Only because he had wanted to venture into a shop in this strange world and a lettuce was all he could think to ask for. The woman had wrapped it in newspaper and then stood chatting with him for ages. The lettuce on the car seat beside him seemed now like a trophy: a prize for being brave.

As he started the car engine the man felt a strange reluctance to be leaving. A place of fear had become a place of human encounter. He wanted to go back and say thank you: but for what? He was seeing this battered fragment of the inner city in a new light.

As he drove home with his lettuce he felt differently about the city and the places where you know you will be mugged – because it is well known and always in the papers.

A DAY IN THE CITY

Other people taking part in the project also had encounters which threw a new light on their city – and challenged some of their assumptions about the values and priorities of western society.

One of the most unlikely parts of the project required the participants to spend a day in the city centre with just £1 to spend. As with the walking meditation, the idea was to experience a little of life as it is lived by other people. It did not pretend that living on £1 for a day would show wealthy people what it was like to be poor: but it was a symbolic way of setting aside their wealth for a few hours, and being alongside people whose lives were stunted by poverty and the lack of choices.

The idea was to spend the day with no other purpose than trying to see the city and its people through the eyes of God, and being attentive to what was happening in this small part of God's world.

After a short briefing session and a few moments of prayer at the city centre church which was being used as their base, the participants went their separate ways to spend a day in the city. Leaving cash, credit cards and cheque books in the church-safe, they would not be allowed back for eight hours.

A woman participant described one incident from her retreat on the streets in the following way:

> The first few hours seemed very artificial: almost exciting. I explored the city as though I was a sightseer, even though I have lived here all my life. I did a lot of walking and eventually my legs began to ache. I suddenly realized that the

day had been planned to run from midmorning to early evening: spanning two meal times. I began to feel a bit uneasy.

I bought a carton of milk and a chocolate bar and sat on a bench in the city square to rest. I watched the people going past. They all seemed to have somewhere to go and things to do and it made me feel a bit useless. Nearby, other people were sitting drinking or begging. They made me uneasy so I walked some more.

Finally I just had to sit down. It had got hotter and my mouth was very dry but I had long since spent my £1. The only place I could find to sit was on some church steps. There was a beggar there as well but I was past caring. He asked if I had twenty pence for a cup of coffee. I could have laughed. I told him I had no money on me.

I thought I would feel bad about not having any money but in an odd way I felt a sense of freedom. As though there were no barriers. For once there was no question about whether to give money to a beggar: I had none to give. Nothing to give: nothing to lose.

We got talking and I was surprised that the man was quite educated. He smelt a bit with that ripe smell of old sweat and his hands were dirty. I remember the nicotine on his fingers and his dirty nails. After a time I actually began to enjoy our conversation. A while later someone stopped and gave him a couple of coins. He got up to go and get another drink. As he stood up his old beer can fell over and rolled across the pavement but it was empty.

I called out goodbye and he shouted something I didn't catch and was gone. I felt a bit lonely on my own. I wondered what God thought of my friend and his beer cans. I looked at my watch: still four hours to go before we were allowed back. What a crazy way to spend a day.

I thought about walking some more to kill time when I suddenly realized my friend was coming back carrying a plastic cup of coffee.

We shared the cup and talked some more. What was I

doing? Where was I from? I felt oddly embarrassed to say I was praying about the city and that I was from a church, but he didn't seem surprised.

For a few minutes he was silent. Then he turned to me and said: 'Most of us on the streets believe in God, you know.'

I mumbled some sort of approving words trying not to sound patronizing but they didn't come out right and he wasn't listening anyway. He was looking out across the street. Maybe looking out across his life. He had a thoughtful, distant expression on his face. He looked very sad.

'Yes, we believe in God,' he said quietly. 'We've got no one else to cry to in the night.'

We sat for a long time and eventually I stopped crying. Crying who for? Crying for him, crying for me, crying for this stupid, selfish world and crying for my stupid, selfish church with its petty bickerings.

Finally he said he had to go. I got up to shake his hand but on impulse hugged him. I smelled the stale beer on his breath; the stubble on his face scratched like my father's did when he hadn't shaved.

'Take care,' he said. 'And God bless you.'

'I don't even know his name,' the woman said later. 'I wish I'd asked him who he was.'

* * *

These two people taking part in their church project had encounters and experiences which they both found profoundly moving and significant. But what if anything does it mean? Are these just isolated incidents, or are other people stumbling across this reality in these strange places and among these unlikely people?

As we look around we find others stumbling on this discovery and catching glimpses of this common reality, both in the events of everyday life – and powerfully and overwhelmingly in the gospels.

The rest of this book is simply a detective story, of other people who are making these discoveries, of how the clues fit together, where they lead, and what they might mean.

And the first clues are a bicycle and a ruined abbey.

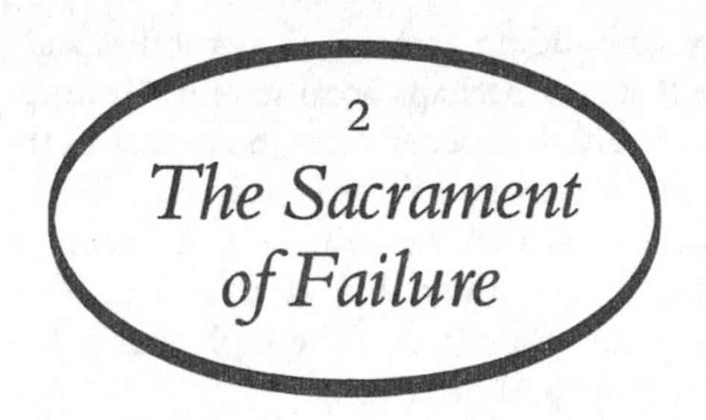

IT HAS BEEN said that the whole is greater than the sum of the parts. A bicycle, for example, is more than a collection of all the different parts that make it up. In addition to all the collected components it is something more: a machine with a function and purpose.

So it would sound contradictory to say that the part can ever be greater than the whole: that anything can be 'more' when it is incomplete than when it is complete.

It may sound contradictory – but it may also be true . . .

Far out in the gentle countryside of the Yorkshire dales stands a ruin called Fountains Abbey. It was built by a community of Cistercian monks back in the twelfth century. The abbey lies in the hollow of a valley, with a river running through the grounds. In its day it was a magnificent example of church architecture – a huge and amazing building in an empty landscape dotted with windswept sheep, and the occasional peasant's cottage.

The towering arches, mighty flying buttresses, superb stained glass windows and magnificent carved woodwork must have been simply awesome to people trying to scratch a living from the land.

But then in the 16th century this mighty edifice was destroyed under the dissolution of the monasteries. Its religious community was scattered, the roof fell in and the windows were smashed. Over the years its stone was looted for local building needs. The abbey became a ruin.

But that was not the end of the story.

The abbey is obviously incomplete today; only a fraction

of the original building remains. It is roofless and wordless, but despite that – or perhaps because of it – its impact on the visitor is probably so much greater today than in those earlier times when it housed a wealthy and closed religious order.

The roof is now the sky and the open walls take in the world where before they shut it out. The stone floor is become grass, and the place of the high altar is empty – but full of significance and presence.

The sun shines down into the open spaces of the great nave and sanctuary, warming the stone as it never could when the abbey was complete. Birds make nests in crevices of the broken stonework. Even the most casual visitor seems moved by the enormity of the damage and the dignity of the remains. There is a sense of stillness and presence.

The abbey will never regain its former greatness. No one will come and restore it to its original state. It will never again be whole or complete. It will always be fragmented, and damaged beyond repair.

No formal monastic worship is likely to take place there as it did in the long distant past. God, even though he was worshipped there, does not undo the damage or recall and reassemble the religious order that built it. But, in a strange way, it may be that God uses the ruin as it is to waken people's minds to the infinite and the holy.

The damaged and incomplete fragment may be greater than the whole ever was; greater than in the days when it was controlled and limited by the mind of man. Tens of thousands of people who would never go near a monastic order or seriously think of God, are drawn to a silence and an encounter not by the wealth and success of the Church, but by an example of its colossal failure and poverty.

The damage and vulnerability of the ruin somehow makes its message more accessible, as though the visitor can enter its story and almost feel compassion; perhaps identifying with feelings of failure and uncertainty in their own lives.

When we are so often cynical and disappointed by the finite, we may be touched by the glimpse of the infinite opened up to us by this fragment of a past age. And what was built to the glory of God may give greater glory in its failure than in its days of success. It is as though the failure becomes a channel for God's love and purpose.

Not only can this happen with buildings, it can also happen with people. Think of a hospice, for example. Anyone visiting a hospice for the first time may feel apprehension before they arrive. People will be terminally ill, and dying. There will probably be crying and pain, depression and despair. Perhaps that is what many people would expect to find.

But most hospices are in reality almost the opposite. People are terminally ill and often dying, but the characteristic mood of a hospice is one of life and of lightness. Patients and relatives are gently and carefully helped to come to terms with the reality of death – but they often find that experience unexpectedly liberating.

In the one place they expected to find darkness and meaninglessness they are surprised to encounter purpose, integrity and even joy. They find that in facing the challenge of death they are brought face to face with life; and discover within themselves an unexpected courage and a deepening of relationships.

Death does come, as it comes to all of us. But when the person has died, friends and relatives often revisit the hospice to carry out voluntary work: gardening, helping to run a gift stall, operating an informal taxi service for other visitors. The place of death which they had naturally dreaded has instead become a focus of meaning and life.

All this could of course simply be a way of trying to avoid the reality of bereavement and the grief of losing a loved one: but it may not be. There is always the sense of loss, but this is not the whole picture either. Like the old abbey, in the ruins of a death comes something quite unexpectedly like life.

Hospital staff often see this strange contradiction when people are very ill. Some years ago a small boy was suddenly diagnosed as having cancer. His condition was terminal. A young and innocent life was being destroyed by a disease that no one could halt.

Friends and family visited him regularly in an attempt to cheer him up and make him feel better. They did what they could although it was always hard to know what to say.

For weeks which gradually became months, his mother stayed with him in the hospital, sleeping in a room near the children's ward. He was just an ordinary little boy and she just an ordinary mother.

But over the months something seemed to happen. The boy did not get better, and the cancer spread steadily through his small thin body. But he changed. He became quiet and thoughtful and seemed wise far beyond his years: day by day he seemed to grow in understanding and in what can only be called love.

His mother also seemed to change: despite the anguish of seeing her child suffer, she showed a courage and a strength that no one had noticed before. She would hold him gently but firmly in her arms for hours as he tried to find a comfortable position to lie in. Talking, touching, laughing and teasing. Always loving.

One day, the vicar visiting the ward walked in to see the mother sitting on the bed with the child across her lap. His mind flashed back to a brief visit to St Peter's in Rome and the statue of Mary cradling the body of the crucified Christ. But it was not the *Pietà*: it was a small boy in hospital with cancer. Or was it both?

As the months went by the visitors began to realize that something strange was happening. Whereas in the early days they had visited the hospital to try to comfort and support the boy and his mother, they increasingly found that the loving and the support was happening in reverse.

Parents of other children with cancer on the ward found they were able to support each other, and gradually the terrible isolation of the suffering was transformed into community and solidarity.

A young nurse was given support and comfort after breaking down in tears: she had worked so many hours and under such pressure, that she suddenly realized she had given dozens of injections and carried out a hundred other important jobs without having the time and space to stop and speak a word of human kindness to a single child. The people under her care were caring for her.

Then one bright frosty October morning the little boy died. Held gently in his mother's arms his breathing slowed. His last breath came like a whisper in a silent and peaceful room. People who had seen a hundred deaths wept with anger at the waste of such a life; and with joy at having been touched by such a deep and gentle person.

Faced with pain and death, where did the sense of meaning and dignity come from? How, in the face of their utter failure to save a poor little boy's life, were they given an encounter which they felt was so enriching and life-giving?

Was it all foolishness – all in the imagination? An escape from the reality and futility of death? Or was the word of life spoken from the lips and eyes of a dying child who counted for nothing in the balance sheets of our clock-faced economy?

The Gift of Laughter

One day, a young woman started going to her local church. With her came her Down's syndrome daughter. The congregation were genuinely pleased, but week by week they felt a sadness that the girl had been born so handicapped and that her life was so limited and incomplete.

After some years the young mother decided that she wanted to be confirmed; and that she would like her daughter to be confirmed with her.

The rather trendy vicar, pleased to explore this unusual possibility, began asking among his clergy colleagues for guidance on how to prepare such a disabled person for confirmation – when that preparation usually meant considerable teaching about the Christian faith; teaching impossible for the Down's syndrome girl.

So, instead of the usual confirmation lessons, the vicar and the young mother planned a series of informal chats during which the three of them would talk in very simple terms about what happened at the church; what the Communion service was like; about friends and friendship; parties and celebrating; about people caring for each other; and maybe about the idea of God.

They made a list of all the different people at the church with their tasks: from the bishop who had recently visited the parish, to the people who cut the churchyard grass. Suddenly they found themselves asking what the young girl's 'job' at the church was. Slightly patronizingly, the vicar said it was to be welcoming and friendly, as indeed she always was.

A week later when they met again there were two surprises for the vicar. He had forgotten to note down the list of people and jobs: but then discovered to his amazement that she could remember them all.

The other surprise was the realization that the 'job' this disabled girl did at church was a real one. Because she seldom hid her feelings and because she was instinctively an open and loving person, she was in truth the most welcoming and friendly person at the church.

Not only that, the vicar had realized that this ministry was probably the most important thing that happened at the church. What people needed when they came was a warm, honest and loving welcome. And this damaged and handicapped girl seemed to be one of the very few people around who were capable of consistently offering that love.

Instead of being regarded as a passenger whom the rest of the congregation tolerated in a kindly way, people began to see that she had a great contribution to make in an area where the church was failing: that of loving people.

So when it came to the confirmation, instead of there being an unspoken apology that a disabled person was being confirmed, there was a sense that something profoundly important was happening: both for her and for the church.

But it did not stop there. Each week after that when she came to the altar to receive the bread and wine, the vicar saw there was an incredible attentiveness and calm in the way she received communion. At the one point in the service where words are unnecessary, the simple act of receiving bread and wine communicated itself to the child in a deep, unspoken way.

The girl was limited in many areas of her life, and in a physical sense she was less than whole. How then was she so important in the life of that church? Comparisons are meaningless, but the one person in that church who would be instantly judged as less than the others, and to be damaged in her personhood, was in reality one of the most profoundly alive and loving.

How ironic that the love of God and such a sense of the presence of God was being channelled through a person so handicapped; one of life's unfortunate failures in terms of worldly success and achievement.

Poor girl, people would say sympathetically. Poor people, thought the vicar, who often wished a few more of the congregation were able to engage with God in the way she did, and to love other people with that same Christ-like directness.

No Place Like Home

Some years ago a middle-aged priest who had for some time been concerned about the increasing poverty and deprivation in many of Britain's cities, suddenly had the offer of a job working alongside homeless people. It was a difficult decision:

frustrations with the institutional church were one thing, but to abandon the security of a full time job was quite another.

Finally he decided to make the change. But in the event his work with homeless people proved less of a trauma than he had feared. The people he met were not what he had expected. Many of them had serious problems with alcohol, and they often had difficulty finding appropriate work, but they did not seem any more or less honest than the people in the average bus queue.

But what he did find was that they were far more welcoming and accepting than many other people he had ministered to.

Ministered to? Still in his mind was the assumption that 'his ministry' was in some way to do good to them. To spread the Good News from him to them by deeds as well as words.

Meanwhile, his attempts to buy a house in the city were proving difficult. The purchase of a small terraced house was delayed and then fell through. There was a death in the family. A second house was found. That, too, was delayed and delayed again. Suddenly he was told he would have to move out of his former clergy house. He had nowhere to go. Where would he live?

He could not afford to rent a house big enough to take his furniture; and he could not afford to rent a smaller house as well as paying to have his furniture in storage. A quiet panic began to set in.

A few days later, one of the homeless people he was working with took the worried priest on one side. Putting an arm round his shoulders the man said: 'Don't worry about the house. If you get stuck you can come and kip with us.'

Who was ministering to whom? Who was proclaiming the Good News to the worried priest? What was good news for him at that moment? It was a place to live. What was the homeless person offering? A place to live. When had the priest ever offered a homeless person a place to live? Never – and the thought had never seriously crossed his mind. Normally he had not even let 'them' get past the front door when they had called at the vicarage.

He thought about what had happened and tried to convince himself that there was a difference between kindness and the love of God. After all, what do homeless people know about God?

Then he remembered the funeral.

FOR THOSE IN PERIL

Funerals can be dangerous places for unsuspecting clergy. A mistaken name or an ill-considered comment can bring disaster. A minister conducting a funeral service for a trawler fisherman found the crematorium was full of bristling seamen.

Rightly assuming that few of them were churchgoers, he began his address with the ill-fated words: 'I don't suppose many of you believe in God . . .'

After the service he was cornered by a group of angry fishermen who told him in very clear terms that, while they might not show up in church every Sunday, they certainly believed in God. And facing death each day on the sea, they probably knew and kept in touch with God a lot more purposefully than he did in the comfort of his study.

A FRIEND OF GOD

Back in the inner city a chance conversation seemed to prove the point. A homeless man who was at that time living in an alcohol rehabilitation unit happened to comment: 'I say my prayers, you know. Night and morning I say them.' He paused and added: 'Then, when I've said them I just talk to God.'

He had no home, no money, no possessions, no church, no status and no future. Just a priceless, natural friendship with God.

As the priest continued to work in the city he began to question what it meant to be a priest. It was an important question for him and there seemed to be no clear answer.

How do we know what we are, and what we are meant to be? Are we meant to be anything? And is there any meaning? What does it mean to be the Church? What does it mean to talk about the 'Good News' and the Gospel? And who is listening? The questions buzzed round his head.

Week by week he worked at a drop-in centre which ran a clothing store for homeless people. People in desperate need of shoes and clothing would come in to see if there was anything that would fit them. And always it was the men's shoes that were in short supply.

One day an elderly man came in asking for shoes. There was a pair, but he needed to try them on to see if they would fit. His own worn shoes were sodden from walking in the rain and the laces were hopelessly knotted.

Without thinking, the priest got down on his knees to help the elderly man, and after a struggle the shoes were untied and removed. As he was helping the elderly man to try on the newer shoes the priest suddenly realized what was happening.

Kneeling at the feet of a homeless elderly man, he had discovered what his ministry was about. He was not remotely pretending to be Christ kneeling to wash the disciples' feet, but that was the picture that came to mind.

Except that it was he rather than the elderly man who was receiving and being loved – but by whom? The elderly man came in looking for a pair of shoes and went out with the shoes; without realizing it, the priest had come in looking for his own identity and meaning. And he went out having received that precious gift.

In this and in many other ways it came home to the priest that he was not bringing God to the homeless: it was the homeless and poor who were living and speaking the love of God to him in his need and his spiritual poverty. It was they who were the outward and visible expression of God's presence.

The Fried Egg Eucharist

Not so long ago, a Catholic sister working alongside homeless people in the same city told a story which put this discovery into sharp focus. She was holding a picnic in a park, to which people who were homeless or living in insecure accommodation were invited.

On the menu as always, were fried egg sandwiches cooked on a small camping gas stove. The last sandwich was being served up by a man who was often homeless himself, and who that day had been doing the cooking. Serving himself last, it may well have been his main meal of the day.

Suddenly, two more men appeared out of the bushes on the other side of the park. Uncertain what to do; they hesitated. But the man with the fried egg sandwich on seeing them, shouted across the grass, 'Come on lads, there's some for you.'

Saying that, he broke the fried egg sandwich in two. The egg yoke broke and spilled out of the bread as he gave it to them.

What was going on there? Nothing more than a shared sandwich. Nothing more than a chance act of kindness. An impulse. An act whose symbolism was in the eye of the beholder: subjective and unreal?

Or was it unreal? In a thousand different and fragmentary ways which are not and cannot be documented, evaluated and processed, a love is being lived by and from people we call the poor. And it sounds and feels disconcertingly like the love lived out by the Christ person: the outward and visible sign of God's presence and purpose among the poor whom he knew.

Life is being experienced in places of death; moss-covered ruins seem to communicate a presence and a reality which a hundred working churches cannot begin to imitate; damaged and handicapped people shine out with a meaning that others never glimpse; the homeless poor offer shelter to a worried priest and, for a moment, live out the meaning of eucharist with a fried egg sandwich, broken and given in a city park.

Perhaps we need to recognize God's love lived out in situations of poverty, rejection and suffering; and even to consider that there may be something which we may call the sacrament of failure. Outward and visible signs of God's life-giving presence made real in the weakness and brokenness of the least of our sisters and brothers.

Instead of being categorized in the world's system of values as worthless and a problem to be solved, those we label the poor could in reality be the only hope we have for life. God, the reference point for all meaning and reality, may be using a very unlikely channel to bring life to a sick world – the powerless poor.

But perhaps with all this talk of fried egg eucharists and unheard of sacraments we are rushing ahead too fast. Maybe we are slipping too hastily into assumptions about God and his concern for the poor. And perhaps we are being too critical of the world in which we live.

What, after all, is so wrong with success, with progress, with our consumer society? We are grown up; we know where we are going; and we know what is real. Or do we?

It may be that the next clue is a greyhound.

ADMITTEDLY, GREYHOUND RACING has never had the glamour and prestige of horse racing, but the excitement and fascination of watching powerful animals pushed to the limit of their physical strength is similar in both sports.

The release of huge and dedicated energy is fascinating: enthralling.

The difference is that the greyhounds have no one to steer them or whip them on in the race. Instead, there is an artificial rabbit or hare which is automatically trailed round the track ahead of the dogs.

As the starting gates spring open the powerful dogs explode onto the track in pursuit of the hare. But, no matter how fast the dogs run through the dust and glare of the floodlights, they will never catch their elusive quarry.

No matter how many races they compete in, the artificial hare always stays ahead. But the dogs never seem to become disillusioned and give up. This is what they are trained to do – and what they are rewarded for doing.

Perhaps they enjoy the excitement of the chase; perhaps it touches a deep primal instinct of the hunt in both dog and spectator, and awakens a long-forgotten pack memory of the wild.

Western society often speaks of people being caught up in a race. We pretend to disapprove of such competitiveness by calling it the rat race.

But for many people, this competitive struggle to be first is a powerful driving force affecting the lives of both adults and children.

Whether in school, in sport, or in our careers, we are under pressure to be winners. We are encouraged to think that human development needs this competition to draw out the best in us: that if we are not competitive we will be lazy, unadventurous and complacent. Above all, we will be inadequate.

But what is the rabbit in our own lives? What is it that we are chasing? Are we chasing anything, or are we running away from our fears of failure and inadequacy? Who is setting the rules of our race; do we really want to run; and at the end of it all, what has been achieved? And by whom and at what cost?

What about the people who are not designed like greyhounds? People who cannot run very fast?

As we leave the starting gate of birth and set out on the journey of life, why are we running? Why are we elbowing other people aside, off the track and into the gutter? Why do we create league tables of achievement, approval and success?

As they run their race at the greyhound track each dog strives to be first; to defeat the other dogs; to achieve an individual conquest and to be the pack leader. Is that what we believe human life should be like? That the individual, the leader, is all – and the community nothing?

Why is it that we assume a powerful car is in some way better then a slower car – even though the slower car may do less damage to the environment? Why is a huge salary the measure of achievement rather than the character of the work being done?

Why is a business tycoon almost universally regarded with admiration, even though one commercial operation may destroy huge areas of vital rain forest, while another causes the deaths of thousands of children every day of the year by its aggressive food-marketing strategies?

Why do we think so little of people who empty our refuse bins or staff the sewage works in every city in our land? These people are likely to be met with laughter and ridicule when they reveal their occupations. Yet theirs is crucial for the health and well-being of us all. They are the important ones.

Why do we so often assume, or allow ourselves to be persuaded, that it is in some way better to be slim, sun-tanned, sexually assertive, expensively dressed, beautiful and intelligent?

Why does our society still degrade women by its violence, its sexism, and its economic discrimination? And why do we so avidly support a media network which often seems committed to entertainment and stimulation rather than the objective communication of information: where comment is mistaken for fact and fantasy is often allowed to replace reality?

What are we doing and why are we doing it? What if anything gives meaning and purpose to this life? What is real and what is illusion? There are times when we seem locked into the greyhound track of life in a race in which we are all losers.

Losers because we dishonour and diminish ourselves by the grievous hurt we often do to others by our apathy and greed. At the end of the day there are no winners: only longer obituaries and more ornate coffins.

We do not want to face this possibility because it is too painful. And, to be honest, most of us are running so hard that we do not have much time for thinking. Thinking about reality, anyway.

We have long since discarded the notion of God: and yet, with a bitter irony, most of us spend our lives worshipping another god: Mammon. We call greed enterprise; and selfishness masquerades as freedom.

So it seems unlikely that in an age of secular rationalism the concept of God has anything to say to us about reality. Indeed, for most people, the idea of God is probably synonymous with an escape from reality and not an engagement with it.

But sometimes we find our missing glasses in the place we are convinced they cannot be: where we have already looked before, or where we least expect them: on the end of our nose.

Perhaps the same may be true of reality, or even God, whom we are convinced cannot exist because we have looked before. And in any case we are grown-up, we have come of age, and we have put away such childish fantasies.

But, no matter how unfashionable it may be, there are people who in a huge leap of faith, or perhaps irrational foolishness, hold that reality and meaning have their source in God. They believe what cannot be proved: that creation is not meaningless and arbitrary but is an expression of the will and purpose of this God.

That, if the world is simply a goldfish bowl of life floating in an empty and random universe, then nothing has any meaning or value. But if there is such a thing as God then meaning and purpose are, and can only be, understood with reference to that God.

At the heart of the Christian faith is the belief that God's creativity and purpose can be known and related to in human terms; that we are called to recognize and respond to God's relationship with the world; and that the character of that relationship can best be described in human terms as one of caring and unconditional love.

Familiarity Breeds Contempt

Most people in Britain in the closing years of the twentieth century would probably claim to know what Christianity was about. Their answers might well produce an amalgam of rules for co-operative behaviour, avoiding violence to others, and expressing consideration and kindness whenever possible.

The reality is that Christianity is not an adult version of the Boy Scout movement – nor is it the religious wing of the National Trust. It is to do with a particular person. Jesus Christ.

But the question for us is not simply whether this person is or is not at the centre of a particular faith system, but whether this person can in any way provide a reference point for our understanding of reality.

And if so, what sort of a reference point are we encountering?

But good detectives always check their clues. So we may well have to set to one side our inherited and half-remembered assumptions about this Christ person, and try to find out for ourselves who he was. Not who other people may want us to think he was.

The question is: who is to say who this Christ person was or is, and what reality he may be revealing to us? Who better than the people who knew him, we may answer. But who are they?

The nearest we can get would seem to be the people whose stories and words are gathered together in the rather untidy documents we call the gospels.

But we have been reading these for years: for centuries, in fact. And we know what they say.

The difference between Sherlock Holmes and Dr Watson was not that they examined different evidence, but that the great detective noticed what the well-meaning doctor missed. He looked at the same evidence but saw different things, and so drew different conclusions.

We need to follow his example and look at some familiar evidence. Imagine you had never heard of the gospels. And remember why we are on this case. We are not seeking a religious sedative to help us through the difficult times in our lives.

We are searching for what is real in life: and what that might have to do with ruined abbeys, bicycles and fried egg sandwiches in the park.

4
Searching For Clues

SOME OF THE most exciting and magnificent words ever written form the first sentences of the document we call St John's Gospel. Probably written about one hundred years after the birth of Christ, they well up like some great ocean breaker into a towering mass of meaning about the deepest things in life.

Then, in a few short sentences they come crashing down in a quite amazing statement of reversal:

> In the beginning was the Word and the Word was with God and the Word was God . . . through him all things were created. In him was life, and that life was the light of men . . . The true light that enlightens every man was coming into the world. He was in the world and the world was made through him, yet the world knew him not. He came into his own realm, but his own people received him not . . . (John 1.1–12).

Having thought long and deeply about who Jesus was, John opens his gospel with the most astounding series of statements which leave us in no doubt as to who he believed Jesus to be.

Writing to an audience who shared a Greek rather than a Jewish culture, John uses a term well-known to his particular audience: Logos – the Word.

In Jesus Christ, says John, we see nothing less than the Word of God in human form: the mind of God, the reason of God, the will of God embodied and expressed in this person.

What is a word? A word is a means of communication; a bridge, a link, an expression of thought and purpose. That, says John, is what is happening in Jesus Christ. That person is the authentic expression of the will, the thought and the mind of God.

For the Jewish community the concept of 'the word of God' also had colossal implications. It was as though the Word of God was a concrete reality; an instrument of God's creativity – an outpouring of directed energy. Rather like an arrow shot from a bow it could not be deflected as it flew towards its target. So in the wonderful creation story in Genesis we read: 'God said . . . and it was so.'

John is not saying that this untidy and rebellious carpenter from a small northern town is simply a good person or an inspired teacher: he is saying that in this person is embodied the whole will and purpose of God for the world.

Put in crude and simplistic terms we could say God is like Jesus: that if we want to know what God is doing and wants done, we need to look at what Jesus is doing and wants done. Jesus Christ, for John, is the one person who makes the will and purpose of God known.

Not content with this, John makes a further vitally important connection: the Word which was in the beginning with God and by which all things were created, is the same Word which is now embodied in this person of Christ, with the declared task of healing a damaged and sinful world. The same creative will of God is there in both events or activities.

To put it bluntly, John is attributing to the person we know as Jesus Christ absolute authority in showing us the will and purpose of God. He does not say that the person of Jesus Christ together with the writings of St Paul and all the other people who had reflected on the will of God (gathered together like a composite committee resolution), constitute the will and purpose of God: his focus is solely on the Christ figure.

It may be of course that St John was totally wrong and misguided, but if we follow through for a few moments the possibility that he was right, where would we find the clearest statement of who this Christ person was?

The answer is that there is no complete and objectively documented account of what Christ was like. The best we can do is to look at the incomplete collection of stories, memories and traditions which have been collected together into the gospels.

Despite attempts by the Church down the ages to tidy things up, faith is not a mathematical formula, exact and capable of proof. There is no guarantee that what we read in the gospels is at any one point the authentic word of Jesus. There are times when the gospel accounts do not square with each other, or something appears so out of character that we find it difficult to believe it to be true in that instance. There are times when we lose the thread.

It would be more convenient if the accounts had been thoroughly edited so as to iron out these problems: convenient but probably less truthful.

All we can say is, that like brush strokes making up a painting, the individual statements of the gospels laid alongside each other and often overlapping, give us a picture which viewed as a whole offers an authentic statement about this Christ person – and about God.

A Rude Awakening

So what happens, then, if we take one of the gospels and simply read it? If a gospel is one of the few source documents available to tell us about the nature and purpose of this Christ person who John thought so important, how does this work out in practice?

What happens if we take for example the earliest gospel, St Mark's, and explore that document? While the Bible as a whole is for many people a hugely intimidating book, Mark's gospel is a mere fragment. Its sixteen short chapters, covering less than thirty pages, can be read easily in an hour.

Mark's gospel may be part of the Bible, but if we expect

the first gospel to be written in the calm and measured tones that we normally associate with formal religion we are in for a rude awakening.

The gospel which has been called the earliest surviving life of Christ, the most important book in the world, and the nearest we shall ever get to an eyewitness account of Jesus, bursts upon the reader like an express train hurtling out of a tunnel.

Its intended readership is a small and persecuted Christian community in Rome at the time of the notorious emperor Nero. They are suffering persecution and martyrdom and Mark is intent on giving them support and encouragement by communicating to them the power and authority of Christ.

The language is unpolished and the style simple, dramatic and even crude. Mark has something urgent to say and he does not waste time in getting to the point. The ideas and accounts are strung together like the carriages of that fast-moving express train.

There is vivid detail; sometimes apparently unnecessary detail, which seems strange in a gospel so short, so urgent and at times so abrasive. Detail which suggests that Mark may have been using eyewitness accounts of events: or may even have been present himself.

Mark writes in a rough Greek but at times lapses into the actual language of Jesus: Aramaic. It may be we hear the very sound of Jesus speaking.

Either because he did not have the time or skill, or because he did not feel it necessary, Mark does not blend the gospel into a well-edited whole: instead he leaves us with isolated statements and events gathered together like photographs pasted into an album.

Perhaps because of the suffering which faced his audience, Mark launches into his gospel with a powerful assertion: 'Here begins the good news of Jesus the Christ, the Son of God.' It is good news not about Jesus the Christ but of Jesus Christ: Christ himself is the content of the good news.

There is news and the news is good: reassuring, even exultant in the face of overwhelming suffering. It is a powerful statement of faith.

In the first dozen words Mark has put down a marker: Jesus is the Messiah, the Son of God: not just a great and good teacher, but above all else the human expression of the power, authority and purpose of God.

For Mark, the title 'Son of God' carries with it the mysterious and awesome overtones of one who will bring about the end of this present age and herald a new order, at the side of which even the might of the Roman Empire pales into insignificance. No matter what the immediate situation may be, there is a greater and over-arching reality.

It is important to keep this opening statement in mind, but in the next sentence Mark suddenly whisks us back into Jewish history with the words: 'In the prophet Isaiah it stands written . . .'

What does an Old Testament prophet have to do with Jesus Christ or with us? And why give this apparently irrelevant statement such huge prominence?

But Mark's reference back to the prophets is crucially important: they were the people who in the face of bitter opposition from the ruling classes of their day would speak the 'Word of God' and call the community back to a true relationship with God.

Often they were persecuted, occasionally they were murdered, and always they were uncomfortably uncompromising people: but despite their bold and angry attacks on the ruling groups of their day, they were always believed by the people to speak with the true voice of God.

With this immediate reference to the prophets, Mark places the Jesus event right inside that uncomfortable but authentic tradition. This person, he is saying, stands within this line of true and courageous men and women: a fact which would be highly significant to his immediate readers.

But we are not allowed to explore this further, and having placed his second marker the gospel surges forward, propelling us through the baptism of Jesus, the temptations of Jesus, the arrest of John the Baptist and the call of Christ's first disciples.

Mark is about important business and he is not about to waste time.

The First Hint of Trouble

Suddenly, a third and discordant element is introduced. Writing what may be the most important book in the world, describing work of universal significance, and addressing a group of frightened people facing all the horrors of arrest and persecution, Mark abruptly changes course.

Without warning, we find him describing Jesus the Christ, the authentic expression of the will of God – as a lawbreaker. He shows him deliberately associating with the lowest in society: the lepers, the outcasts, the mentally ill.

Not only is he associating with these people, but he defies the religious law in order to do so. Still in the first chapter of his gospel and before the ink has dried on the opening monumental statement about who Jesus is, Mark describes him breaking the sabbath law and coming into conflict with the religious authorities by healing a man in a synagogue.

At breakneck speed, Mark leads us through a succession of healing miracles until suddenly we are confronted with a leper (Mark 1.40–5).

ASKING THE IMPOSSIBLE

Besides being an appallingly disfiguring disease, leprosy represented absolute ritual uncleanliness, and demanded total segregation from the rest of the community for religious as well as social reasons. Not only that, leprosy was considered to be utterly incurable. It was said to be as easy to raise the dead as it was to cure a leper.

Despite that, the leper kneels before Jesus and begs for help: 'You can cleanse me,' he says. And Jesus, filled with passionate anger, not at the impertinence of the leper but at the sight of his suffering, in 'warm indignation' heals him.

'Be clean again,' he says.

But in that brief and powerful story three things have happened: The leper, despised and rejected by his fellow human beings, sees in Jesus the power to do what everyone else says is impossible: 'You can cleanse me,' he says. Jesus is recognized as the Christ by the lowest form of human life: the good news that Jesus is the Christ is spoken by the poorest of the poor. From within the rotting flesh of the leper come the words of life.

Second, Jesus does not say 'be clean,' he says 'be clean again.' You have been whole before; you are not a leper; you are a priceless human being who has a disease called leprosy. Jesus acknowledges, affirms and honours the humanity of the person before he heals him.

But perhaps most importantly of all, before Jesus has spoken even a word to the leper, he does something shocking and outrageous: he touches him. And in that simple act of ordinary love and human compassion a colossal barrier is smashed.

To touch a leper is to be instantly defiled. No holy or righteous person must allow themselves to be defiled – because that would be to exclude themselves from a right relationship with God and from the rest of the worshipping community. In that instant says Mark, Jesus the Christ, the Son of God, is himself defiled. It is as if in that moment he has willingly become, in religious terms if not in medical terms, a leper himself.

But how can this be if he is supposed to be the authentic expression of the purpose and will of God? Can God be a leper? Can God break the religious law? What is Mark saying? What is going on here?

But we are not given time to consider the answer before Mark is urging us forward once again into one of the most amusing and at the same time most serious events in the gospel.

A paralysed man is brought to Jesus in the hope of being healed (Mark 2.2–12). He is carried on a stretcher by his friends. But when they arrive at the house where Jesus is speaking they find such a crowd that they cannot get near.

In desperation and with great ingenuity they carry the paralysed man up the outside staircase onto the flat roof of the house. Unfortunately there is no record of the words that pass between them as they struggle to carry the stretcher up the open flight of stairs.

Then having reached the top they break a hole through the roof; through the ceiling into the room where Jesus is speaking. They then proceed to lower their friend down on his stretcher in front of Jesus.

For centuries this story has been read in churches with a hugely false solemnity. Is it a real story about real people? Is it a real story about real roofs and ceilings? Did it happen as Mark describes?

The Fatal Words

Real roofs and ceilings often involve large quantities of rubble, dust, plaster, cobwebs and spiders. Mark is presenting a picture of the Son of God and a large number of interested followers packed into an ordinary Palestinian house all looking up to see what is happening: and all getting covered in large quantities of dust, cobwebs and confusion. Have we ever thought how large a hole it would require for a stretcher to be lowered through it?

Maybe there was a large sliding panel; maybe there was no dust or cobwebs. But how Jesus must have laughed (and perhaps coughed) as the paralysed man was lowered down; and how gladly and with what affection he must have spoken the fatal words: 'My son, your sins are forgiven.'

Why fatal words? Fatal because as the watchful lawyers who were apparently present rightly argued: that is blasphemy. Only God can forgive sins. And blasphemy was an offence punishable by death.

Moments later Mark presents us with another simple but crucial story which may seem commonplace, but to the people of his own day was beyond belief (Mark 2.15–17).

Jesus is described as sharing a meal in the company of many bad characters: people who were regarded as sinful. Even in our own day we instinctively choose to share food with friends, and to invite someone even to have a cup of tea is a clear sign of friendliness and goodwill.

In the society in which Jesus lived the sharing of food was an even more significant statement about friendship, trust and acceptance. To share food with someone was to proclaim that they were a trusted and accepted friend.

But Jesus deliberately sat and shared food with 'sinners' with whom no respectable or religious person could possibly be in fellowship. Instantly, his behaviour is challenged by the religious authorities who demand to know how this holy person can be eating with people they regard as evil.

But instead of backing down and apologizing for his scandalous behaviour, Jesus uses the situation to make a benchmark statement about the purpose of his ministry: 'It is not the healthy who need a doctor but the sick; I did not come to invite the virtuous people but sinners,' he says.

It is a statement which signs his death warrant: the crucifixion begins on page three of Mark's gospel. There is no turning back. Jesus is committed to a course of action which will end in his death.

The Gathering Storm

Although we are still in the opening pages of his gospel account, Mark has already brought us face to face with the three key elements in the life of Jesus: that Jesus is the Christ and speaks the authentic word of God; that this word is specifically one of unconditional love for the sinner, the poor and the outcast; and that this word is in conflict with the religious hierarchy, whose understanding of the will of God is radically different.

By standing alongside the poor and the sinful as Mark remorselessly shows him to be, Jesus places himself on a direct and inevitable collision course with the religious authorities.

Mark is saying that this person whom he presents as nothing less than the embodiment of the will of God chooses to accept, touch and be defiled by people counted as sinful and worthless.

This, he is saying, is at the heart of what Jesus is about: and hence at the heart of God's concern.

Church hierarchies may appear to present Jesus as an essentially passive and mild-mannered person, but the Jesus we encounter in Mark's rapid and fragmentary sketches is far from mild or passive. There is a deep anger against the oppression and injustice he encounters among the poor, and a willingness to engage in open conflict with the oppressors, no matter what the risk may be to himself.

Challenged over his fellowship meal with the 'sinners', Jesus not only affirms that his purpose is about healing and restoring the sick and the downcast, he warns his self-righteous religious critics that 'I did not come to invite virtuous people.'

Again and again in the gospels we see Jesus telling the proud religious dignitaries of his day: 'These sinners will enter heaven and not you.'

Those who assume their future passage with God is booked are told that they have excluded themselves from life. Not because of a vengeful and arbitrary decision by God, but because their arrogance and heartlessness has blocked out the life-giving love which was God's gift to them.

As we are swept forward through Mark's gospel we see Jesus again and again taking time – valuable, crucial time – to be with the poor and the outcast.

But alongside this Mark never forgets his important opening statement about the authority and meaning of Jesus.

Challenged repeatedly over breaking the sabbath law he shows Jesus daring to overturn that law with the words: 'The sabbath was made for man not man for the sabbath: therefore the Son of Man is sovereign even over the sabbath.'

The one who is shown as having the authority of God is at the same time the one declaring God's love, healing and forgiveness for the outcast and the poor. Those excluded and degraded by the very religious system which had always sought to serve God. Its critical failure was that it increasingly attempted to serve God through a system of obedience and purity which was humanly impossible to sustain, rather than through an openness to love which was the essence of God's intended relationship with the world.

5
Good News for the Poor

WE HAVE SPENT a lot of time talking about 'the poor', but who exactly are these people? What do we mean by the poor?

In our own society our concept of 'the poor' can often be charged with overtones of judgement: approval and disapproval. And there is often at least a hint of relief that we, for all our faults, are not as they are.

We accept that the poor of the 'third world' are probably poor through no direct fault of their own and we may therefore regard them as justified in asking for help from the richer nations. In many ways they are the acceptable poor.

But the poor in our own country tend to evoke a different response. Perhaps because they are here alongside us on our own streets and sleeping in our own shop doorways, we have a significantly different attitude to them.

They are often condemned as being work-shy, lazy, and an unnecessary drain on the nation's resources. Beggars are treated with contempt and suspicion, and people who are homeless as if they have deliberately brought their misfortunes on themselves.

Because poverty often evokes a sense of guilt in richer members of society we are tempted to defend ourselves with a pre-emptive strike of judgement and condemnation. The argument probably runs: the poor have often brought their sufferings on themselves; if so, then it is their fault; and if it is their fault it cannot be our fault. So we, the better off, are not to blame for this situation.

We shield ourselves from uncomfortable questions about accessibility of affordable housing; adequate mental health provision; and the effects of unemployment on the low-skilled and on their families.

But who are the poor? Who are the poor in the gospel narratives? Who are the poor we see being befriended by Jesus Christ? As we read the Bible in our western churches it is as though we categorize the 'gospel poor' in the same sort of way that we think of the poor in the traditional pantomime: poor but honest; poor but noble; poor but clean; poor but sanitized and free from any moral blemish. The 'pantomime poor' are attractive and non-threatening of our lifestyles – but they are unreal.

If the gospel poor were similarly unreal, then the statement attributed to Jesus that God had sent him 'to announce good news to the poor' is also unreal and meaningless. But if Jesus came explicitly to bring good news to the 'real poor', then perhaps that good news was for the very people whom we see despised and condemned in our own tabloid press and by our own politicians.

We have already seen in the early chapters of Mark that Jesus accepted, cared for, healed and befriended the outcasts of society. We have also seen how this love and acceptance placed his life in danger and led to his eventual arrest and execution.

It could be argued that some of these gospel situations were isolated incidents: an instinctive response to need and suffering. Perhaps they were no more than an impulsive gesture by a headstrong and idealistic young person.

Where are the examples of Jesus proclaiming good news for the poor in a considered and deliberate way? If this man was who Mark and John claimed him to be, where are the examples of him deliberately linking the supposed will and purpose of God with a real concern and love for the poor?

We will explore four situations which seem to answer this challenge. The first is the story in Mark of a woman suffering from a haemorrhage. And here, in what must surely be one of the most dramatic and agonizing stories in literature, Mark presents us with a double tragedy (Mark 5.21–43).

The Double Tragedy

Jesus is on the lakeshore. Hundreds of people are gathered round him. Suddenly a very important person bursts through the crowd and falls at his feet. The man's name is Jairus and he is the president of the local synagogue.

His little daughter is critically ill and at the point of death; despite being a very important and powerful person he has come in desperation to beg Jesus for his help. Immediately Jesus sets off with the distraught Jairus on their urgent mission.

But as they push their way through the crowd a woman touches the edge of Jesus' robe. He senses that something has happened. He stops and asks who it was who touched his robe. His disciples react with immediate and natural exasperation: does it matter who touched his robe? A hundred people could have touched him in that crowd. They have far more important things to do. They must get to the bedside of this important man's daughter as quickly as possible.

But Jesus insists on stopping and turns round in the crowd to seek out who it was. Then the woman who is trembling with fear comes forward and tells Jesus all that has happened.

For twelve years she has suffered with haemorrhages which have ruined her life: not only has she been physically dragged down by this affliction, but because of the religious laws of purity she has been ritually unclean. An outcast.

All the years she might have hoped for happiness, children and respect, she has suffered a living death. She has spent all her money on expensive medical advice but to no avail. Then, unnoticed in the crowd she has managed to touch the robe Jesus is wearing in a desperate act of faith. And in that moment she has been healed, says Mark.

Despite the angry protests of the disciples, Jairus, and the crowd; Jesus gives her his whole attention and continues the conversation. 'My daughter,' he says, 'go in peace free for ever from this trouble. Your faith has cured you.'

But as he is speaking these words of life and freedom to

her, disaster strikes. From the house of Jairus the president of the synagogue comes the terrible news: his little girl has died.

Jairus must have been on the verge of madness and despair at that moment. His treasured child is dead. But suddenly Jesus intervenes with words we have just heard used in connection with the unnamed woman: 'Have no fear,' he says, 'Only have faith.' And together they resume their futile journey to the house where the child is lying.

When they arrive they are met, not surprisingly, with bitter contempt by the child's family. What took you so long? they seem to be saying. But Jesus tries to calm them: 'Why this crying? The girl is not dead; she is asleep.' But they laughed at him.

Whether the little girl who is twelve years old is asleep or dead we cannot know, but Jesus revives her and she is restored to her family.

Hidden Messages

What does it all mean? Does it mean anything? Apart from being a very exciting story and apart from telling us that Jesus may have been a great healer, the narrative is loaded with unspoken messages: did Mark include it in his gospel for that reason?

What are the hidden messages? Where are the clues? Look at what happens . . .

In one complex narrative we see not just two healing miracles but a profound attack on religious oppression, sexual discrimination, and the idea that status buys special treatment from God. It turns upside down the social, economic and political values of the day. And it tells us something profoundly important about how God brings life out of situations of weakness and failure.

Jairus, the honoured and dignified religious leader in the community, is brought to a point of powerlessness and despair by the illness of his daughter. In desperation he comes down from his high social standing to literally throw himself at the feet of an itinerant preacher, who seems dedicated to discrediting the very religious system Jairus represents.

Meanwhile, the woman approaches Jesus secretly. She is given no name and as an unclean outcast she is the lowest person in that society. All her adult life has been one of despair because of the rules imposed by the religious authorities – personified by the president of the synagogue, Jairus. It is the power structure that he represents and upholds that has condemned this woman to a living death.

All her money has been spent trying to be made whole and clean, but now her savings and resources are gone: and like Jairus she is completely powerless and in despair.

Even so, her problem is in no way as critical as that of the dying little girl. Reason dictates that she should wait. Jesus could always come back and speak to her later when the time is more appropriate. But, even after she has touched his robe and known herself to be healed, Jesus insists on stopping to acknowledge her.

He seeks her out, creating a space even in this dire situation to recognize her as a human being – a person of infinite worth. As well as healing and compassion there is a great courtesy in this situation.

Jesus speaks the words of good news to her: 'You are healed. You have been healed by your faith in God. And your healing is permanent. You are free. You have received life.'

But in the instant that she receives life and is called 'my daughter' by Jesus, it is as though poor Jairus has precious life torn from him with the message: 'Your daughter is dead.'

The daughter who was dead because of the religious laws is alive – and the daughter who was alive has died.

Even then Mark has not finished with us. Jesus says he still wants to go to the house of Jairus. But two things have happened: first Jesus has been touched by an unclean woman and so is ritually defiled himself. That being so, how can he enter the house of the president of the synagogue without defiling the whole house? Second, the little girl is dead, and the man who could have saved her life is the last person on earth that the family will want to see: hence the bitter contempt and scornful laughter that greet him.

But amazingly, Jairus agrees. He will trust Jesus even though there can be no chance of his daughter being saved. For some reason he will disobey his own religious law – the law of God – to allow Jesus to enter his home.

Moments later the daughter is restored. How significant that Mark reports the fact that the girl was twelve years old. The unnamed woman had been denied life by the religious law imposed by the girl's father for exactly the same length of time that the little girl had been living a life of happiness, wealth and privilege only a few streets away.

With Empty Hands

It is as though Jesus is saying that the poor who have been denied so much will receive special honour in the new order, and that the rich and powerful will receive life only when they are able to receive it: that is, when they are empty. It is as though they cannot receive the gift of life as long as their hands are full of misused power and privilege which damages others. The poor are imprisoned by their material poverty and Jesus has come to proclaim freedom from that captivity. But perhaps the rich are also imprisoned by possessions and by the damaging use of their power.

In this story Jesus deliberately gives special attention to the woman and for the moment ignores the greater need of the man; a strange decision in a society where women were regarded as hugely inferior to men.

Jesus proclaims good news to the poor: first to the woman who has always lived in poverty, and then to the privileged and wealthy Jairus the moment he too recognizes and accepts his own powerlessness and parental poverty.

The story which has within it so much anguish and grief ends with the laughter of those who have been to the depths of despair, and who have been given new life.

And perhaps we also begin to see another strange possibility emerging here in a vague and fragmentary way. Was it not the action of the poor woman in interrupting Jesus on his journey to the house of Jairus that not only led to the death of the daughter but also led Jairus to make a crucial decision about the deadening rules of his religious system?

Was it not her courage which indirectly led him to die himself in the death of his daughter – and to receive life in a far more meaningful way than if his daughter had simply been cured as Jairus had asked? Was not a new discovery of life granted to Jairus and his family through the poor woman? And was that not a new reality they were discovering?

Is Mark's story true? Were there originally two stories which Mark or someone else combined into a composite narrative? Did it really happen? There is no way of knowing for certain.

All we do know is that from a very early point in the life of the primitive Church this story was presented as a true representation of the character and priorities of this Christ person. And this was at a time when many hundreds of people were alive who could clearly remember that person and many of the things he said and did. At least it must have been typical of the values and the reality being lived out by him: at the ultimate cost of his own life.

This new reality would have seemed so revolutionary in its religious, economic, and political implications; that it can hardly have been included in the gospel casually, or without a very clear knowledge of its purpose.

The War of Words

If the story of Jairus and the woman with the haemorrhage is offered to us as an example of an event which shows us Jesus living out a new concept of God and a new relationship with those we call the poor, then what about his teachings?

What did the Christ person have to say about this most

important subject which seems to have been at the centre of his whole life and purpose?

One of his favourite ways of teaching was the parable. There are instances where parables are presented as being a way of hiding the truth from the public at large but, if they were spoken in the form in which we have received them, it seems inconceivable that they were not used as a very effective general teaching method.

But the parables were much more than a collection of stories. First, the parables are called the parables of the Kingdom because they are reckoned to be statements not just about human life, but about the nature of God's rule, or sovereignty, or will. The parables are thought to be ways in which Jesus taught about the character of God and the relationship between God and the world.

Whenever we hear a parable, the crucial question to be asked is: what does this say about the will of God and about God's relationship with us?

The second important feature of the parables is that they tell an action story in which the exact words are not always crucial to our understanding. Some do not depend on any reported words, and are so simple that their accurate transmission is almost guaranteed.

Take for example, the parable of the lost sheep. One sheep strays from the flock, and the shepherd leaves the other ninety-nine to search for the lost animal. There are no spoken words, but what does that story suggest about the poor and the lost? And perhaps about those who stayed safe within the sheepfold: the sheepfold was a typical way of speaking about the religious community.

Third, parables were a characteristic of the teaching ministry of Jesus: they were special to him. That means we are likely to see in the parables the authentic, authoritative teaching of Jesus the Christ – the person whom the gospel writers were convinced was the embodiment of the will and purpose of God himself. So the parables should carry a special weight in our attempt to understand the priorities and concerns of Jesus.

The fourth point to remember is that the parables were not gentle Sunday School stories. They were often shocking to the people who heard them, and often revealed an open conflict which had developed between the religious hierarchy and Jesus.

If we overlook this violence and conflict then we shall not be true to their message: the reality to which this Christ person was pointing.

Brought up in a religious environment which allows us to assume that the parables are no more exciting than a cup of tea, it comes as a surprise to find that in the hands of an often passionately angry young man called Jesus they were dynamic and often violent in their implications.

Moving for a moment from the gospel of Mark to the gospel of Luke we find one of the best-known parables. It is commonly called the Prodigal Son – but the title is somewhat misleading as we shall see.

Luke presents Jesus in a typical situation: eating and drinking with sinners and being fiercely criticized by the religious authorities for doing so.

In response Luke says that Jesus tells a parable: 'He answered them with a parable . . .' In fact, Luke's account shows Jesus firing a salvo of parables at his religious opponents. And the last he tells is the most violent and damning: the Prodigal Son (Luke 15.11–32).

Jesus appears to deliberately lure his listeners into a false sense of security in order to make his revolutionary teaching about God more effective and memorable; and for good measure he does this twice in the one story.

THE REBELLIOUS TEENAGER

There is a farmer who has two sons. Both are due to inherit when the father eventually dies but the rebellious younger son, impatient for his money and unwilling to remain as part of the family, demands his share now.

With a sad heart the father gives him his share and the younger son leaves for a distant land; not even remaining in the same country. Once there, the son spends all the money in reckless living – only to be caught in a severe recession. He is reduced to working on a foreign farm as a labourer looking after the pigs. This was an occupation which would result in his ritual defilement – assuming that his wild living had not already done so.

Finally, the rebellious son is brought so low that he decides to swallow his pride and return home. He knows he cannot ask to be reinstated as a son, but he will ask his father to allow him to work as a paid servant on the family farm.

There must have been a rising sense of expectation as the crowd listening to the parable guessed the judgement about to fall on the rebellious and selfish son: in their law a rebellious son could be stoned to death for bringing dishonour on the family.

What would happen to this one when he arrived home disgraced, penniless, filthy and defiled? Had the father not been nursing his wrath to keep it warm – ready to unleash it on his wicked son?

But Jesus has set a trap for his listeners. While the son is still a long way off, the father sees him. Is this by chance or has he been looking out for him each day he has been gone?

But instead of waiting with justifiable indignation for the son to arrive at the door, the father runs to meet him. To the horror of the crowd listening to the parable, who are naturally expecting anger and condemnation, before the son can utter a word the father flings his arms round him and kisses him.

The boy begins to make his prepared speech acknowledging that he is no longer fit to be his son. But instead of punishing his son the father tells his servants: 'Fetch a robe, my best one, and put it on him. Put a ring on his finger and shoes on his feet.'

Then he calls for a great celebration because the son he thought was dead is alive; he that was lost is found.

That father, Jesus seems to be saying, is how God is. That unconditional love and forgiveness and delight in the safe return of a lost child, is the nature of the relationship that God has with all of us.

The crowd might well have been surprised at the picture of a respectable and wealthy father figure actually hitching up his robes and running down the dusty road to meet his sinful son. Some of them might well have been horrified that such a person would physically touch someone who was so obviously defiled, and thereby become defiled himself.

They might well have been outraged that instead of well-deserved punishment the selfish and greedy son should be treated so royally: the robe was the symbol of honour, the ring was the symbol of authority, and the shoes were the sign that the boy was a son and not a slave. He deserved none of those things.

Their indignation would not simply have been at the story but at the fact that Jesus, increasingly recognized as a teacher and healer of authority, was stating this with approval: as though to say that this is how it should have been.

But there is worse to come.

The elder brother, who as such will inherit two-thirds of the family wealth under the law, is in the fields working. He hears the celebrations and demands to know what is happening. When he is told that his brother has returned he is angry and refuses to go in.

His father comes out and pleads with him, but the elder son refuses and turns on the father in a bitter attack. 'I have slaved for you all these years and carried out every order you have given,' he says. 'But now this son of yours after wasting your money with his women comes back and you throw a party for him.'

The father pleads again: 'Your brother was dead but has come back to life. How could we help celebrating?' But the story ends with the elder brother still unreconciled – and still outside.

Jesus is saying that the loving father had two sons who were both dead: one dead because he had gone away and seemed lost forever; the other dead because of the sterile relationship of obedience and resentment he seems to have had with the father: obedient in every detail but without a hint of love.

He can find no love for his brother either: he refers to him as 'your son' refusing even to admit that he himself has a blood relationship with him, and bitterly resenting the fact that his brother has had a good time with the share of the inheritance. In the end, his hatred is so great that he prefers to stay outside, rather than go inside the house to join the party and acknowledge the younger son as his brother.

It would not have been lost on the religious authorities that the elder brother's loveless and lifeless obedience to the law, and the forgiveness and love of the father for the sinful younger son was a fair reflection of how Jesus saw their relationship to the poor and outcast, and to God.

This was not a pleasant Sunday sermon on rebellious teenagers or on the merits of being a good parent: it was a powerful attack on a repressive religious system and a devastating condemnation of those who operated that system.

And this is presented in the gospel not as the personal opinion of an unusual religious teacher: it is presented as a definitive statement on the reality of God by the one person recognized as being the embodiment of the will and purpose of God.

How strange, and how offensive to the religious authorities, that the younger brother, although losing all the material possessions he had, nevertheless through his foolishness and sinfulness comes to a far deeper relationship with the father than the elder brother – far deeper than if he had stayed at home.

It is in the poverty of his misdeeds that he unexpectedly discovers the priceless gift of love. Leaving home impatient, selfish and wealthy he in reality has nothing: returning disgraced, penniless and covered in the filth of pigs he is gifted with everything.

The story of the prodigal son or the loving father seems to express very forcefully that the love of God is good news for the poor: even when the poor are selfish and undeserving as in reality, being only human like the rest of us, they often are.

6 Problems With Neighbours

IF REALITY INVOLVES God, and if the Christ person is the one who shows us the nature of this God, then the parables may be vital clues in our search. The parables may indeed be defining statements of reality.

In the parable of the prodigal son we are being told about the essential nature of God in relationship to the world: its wealthy and its poor, the prudent and the reckless, the successful and the failures.

But God's relationship to the world is not something that we can possess: it is not a cosy one-to-one relationship between the individual and God. It involves other people. The problem is that Jesus summed up the relationships that constitute reality by saying, not just that we must love God with all our heart, but that we must also love our neighbour as we love ourselves.

The two parts of the commandment are not separable: you can't have the first part without the second. That would be like saying: 'Love me; hate my child.' The reality of being human embraces both. If the first part of the commandment is illustrated in the parable of the prodigal son, the implications of the second and equally essential part are described in that other well-known parable: the good Samaritan (Luke 10.30–7).

But before we look at this story, perhaps we need to remind ourselves that in the parables Jesus is not handing out moral guidelines in theoretical situations: he is speaking in the real world about how the essential nature of reality is to be explored.

This reality is about the love of God: but love is not a static concept. Love is a social activity that happens in concrete situations between human beings – or doesn't happen at all.

When we come to this well-known parable, we are once again in danger of allowing familiarity to breed contempt. Once again we need to remember this is not a Sunday School story but part of an on-going conflict between the religious authorities and Jesus.

THE LAWYER'S TEST

The story begins with a lawyer, not asking for spiritual guidance as may first appear, but putting Jesus to the test. 'What must I do to inherit eternal life?' he asks. A very serious contest has begun – rather like a game of chess. The voices are polite and the tones measured: but a battle is being waged.

'You know the law,' replies Jesus, 'what does it tell you?'

'Love God with all your heart, mind and strength, and love your neighbour as yourself,' answers the lawyer.

'That is correct,' Jesus says, 'do that and you will live.'

The preliminary moves are over but the lawyer has set a trap for Jesus. The lawyer, Jesus, and the crowd all know the commandments to love: that is not what the conversation is about.

'But who is my neighbour?' asks the lawyer persistently.

We are not sure what the lawyer's precise intention is. It may be to trap Jesus into defining neighbour as someone the law would not accept: to show Jesus yet again as a breaker of the law of God and therefore a bogus and heretical teacher not to be trusted. After all Jesus was a good neighbour to many people defined as being outcast and beyond God's love.

It is as though the lawyer is trying to lure Jesus into making a mistake, in defining a category of 'neighbour' which is against the law.

But Jesus does not define a category. Instead he describes an event. But now it is he who is setting the trap. On the face of it the story would be familiar to his listeners.

A foolhardy person travelling alone on a notoriously dangerous stretch of road is attacked, robbed, and left for dead. Down the road comes a priest, who, as everyone listening will know, has a religious duty to help such a victim. But even though he sees the wounded traveller he passes by on the other side of the road.

Then another religious official, a Levite, comes along the road. He too sees the wounded traveller and passes by on the other side.

But, says Jesus, a Samaritan passing down that road sees the wounded man, and he has compassion on him and rescues him.

Then Jesus challenges the lawyer by asking: 'Which of the three proved to be neighbour to the wounded traveller?' The lawyer is forced to acknowledge that it was the one who showed compassion.

'Go and do likewise,' says Jesus.

The parable of the Samaritan who had compassion has been used to teach that we must love our neighbour: regardless of who that neighbour may be. That our neighbour is any and every person who has a need of our love. And who does not have a need of love? The Samaritan was a person hated by the society in which Jesus lived. The parable emphasizes that love must not be restricted to legal or national categories or notions of liking or social acceptance. Our enemy is also our neighbour.

It teaches that people fail in their duty, as the priest and Levite did in not stopping to help: probably in case the wounded man was dead and they became defiled by his corpse – and thus unable to fulfil their religious duties. It teaches that religious leaders are often hypocrites in preaching one morality but living another.

The parable shows that love is a living relationship: that the priest and the Levite saw and turned away; but the Samaritan, the enemy, saw and had compassion.

It echoes the teaching of Jesus: love your enemy and bless those who hate you.

A Hidden Warning

It may be that Jesus intended this to be a teaching situation and that the crowd, even though they were hearing an already familiar law spelled out to them, would gain a new and deeper insight.

But it may be that something even more significant and disturbing is being said in this seemingly polite and innocent situation.

The lawyer is a custodian of the religious law: six hundred different regulations drawn up to show people how to respond rightly to God. And they must all be obeyed. It may be that the original intent behind this legal structure had been good, but the reality was an overwhelming legalistic burden which hindered an open and loving relationship with God.

Instead of being about love, that relationship had increasingly become a matter of obedience: of religious performance.

In the eyes of the world, the people who fulfilled God's will were the successful religious performers: holy people who carefully obeyed every nuance of the law of God. But the reality was different: the reality, said Jesus, was a man lying injured in the road. The reality was the custodians of the law of God denying the love of God and walking past.

The reality was a hated foreigner, an outcast, fulfilling the law of God by acting with love and compassion.

The point of the parable is not that the Samaritan was good and saved the traveller, but that it was the outcast Samaritan who lived out the reality of God's love, when the priest and Levite had failed to do so. He, and not they, had fulfilled God's will.

Jesus is saying that the will of God cannot be defeated or

diverted. Like the arrow it flies to its target. And if those who were originally chosen to do God's will do not fulfil that mission, then others will be chosen to replace them. It is as though God is saying that the man attacked and left for dead is my child – and if you, the religious custodians of my law, will not love him then I will find others who will.

And if that applies to the man who fell among thieves in the story, then perhaps it also applies to all those who are victims of violence, abuse, discrimination, and sickness: many of whom Jesus befriended in real life.

The confrontation ends with Jesus telling the lawyer: 'Go and do likewise.' But this is not a gentle moral murmur of guidance: it is an ultimatum. Go and live the love of God as the Samaritan did: change your whole system of repressive legalistic power and control and become a servant – or you will be swept aside.

What was the good news for the wounded traveller? It was someone saving his life, rescuing him from his dire predicament. But by whom was that good news spoken? In both words and in actions by the outcast Samaritan.

In the face of the failure of the powerful, educated, wealthy, established religious élite, the love of God was instead channelled to the wounded and powerless through the despised and the outcast. Instead of the good news of life being channelled through the religious, Jesus describes it as being channelled through people who were, in their different ways, the poor.

But it must have been very difficult for the powerful religious élite to grasp what was being said. They, like many of us, had been brought up in a religious tradition in which you inherited ideas and assumptions about God – and probably seldom questioned them. It must have been confusing to say the least when they encountered this Christ person.

Experiencing some of those confusions ourselves, we may feel sympathy for those in the gospel accounts who seemed unable to grasp what was going on.

There is a brief account in the gospel of Luke (18.9–14), which describes such a situation, and which can be read in one of two ways. It is either a very harsh and uncompromising account of Jesus in conflict with his opponents: or it is a situation in which Jesus sorrowfully points out the consequences of pride and arrogance among the religious élite.

However, as Luke prefaces his story of the parable of the sinner in the temple by saying it was 'aimed at' those who were sure of their own goodness and who despised other people, it may be that Jesus was not being particularly sorrowful on this occasion.

Either way, it is a fascinating example of Jesus pointing to the unexpected reality of life: and showing how the poor, this time in the form of the explicitly sinful poor, can offer the possibility of life to others by the very words that they speak. Perhaps we need to listen more attentively . . .

Two people go up to the Temple to pray. One is a Pharisee and the other a tax-gatherer. The Pharisee stands up and prays: 'I thank you God that I am not like the rest of men; greedy, dishonest, adulterous, or for that matter like this tax-gatherer . . .' And he continues to tell God what a splendid person he is.

But when it is the tax-gatherer's turn to pray, he keeps his distance and will not even raise his eyes to heaven. He simply prays: 'O God, have mercy on me, sinner that I am . . .'

But to the consternation of his listeners, Jesus tells them that it was the tax-gatherer who went away acquitted, and not the Pharisee.

The Question of Sin

This parable has been called one of the parables on prayer: but the fact that the two men are formally praying is less important than the issue of honesty. It is about distinguishing between self-deception and reality.

The Pharisee is being dishonest with God and with himself when he adopts his holier-than-thou attitude. He would have been familiar with Psalm 143 which pleads: 'Enter not into judgement with your servant, Lord, for in your sight no one is innocent . . .'

But swept along on a wave of self-righteousness, the Pharisee first boasts of his own holiness and then pours contempt on the people who do not match his performance levels. His concept of being right with God is one of obedience to the religious law: and anyone who does not conform to those laws is by definition a sinner. And, while we may not care very much for his manner and lack of courtesy to others, we may have some sympathy with that general view.

But the parable leaves us in no doubt that Jesus saw things differently: and that he may have had a radically different view of sinfulness to that of the Pharisee – and maybe to that which we have inherited.

He seems to be saying that sinfulness is not so much a matter of breaking a law as of damaging a relationship. And that means a relationship with God and with other people. A sin is something which blocks, hinders, damages or denies a relationship of love.

We can test out this theory very easily by asking whether Jesus ever sinned. And the answer, in terms of disobedience to the law, is of course that he did. The gospels are deliberately littered with accounts of him doing what was considered sinful and against the law: healing people on the sabbath, allowing his disciples to pick ears of corn on the sabbath, not bothering to wash his hands before eating food.

And so it seems that to Jesus, sin was not primarily about obedience to a set of religious laws.

But the Church talks about Jesus taking away the 'sin' of the world. How can "the world' have sinned? What does this mean? It means that Jesus in some way removes a blockage between the world and God: it is about the healing of a relationship, building a bridge across a gap, creating and affirming a life-giving relationship of love.

The irony of the parable of the Pharisee in the Temple was that in the very act of boasting about his sinlessness, he denied himself an open and honest relationship with God. He sins in the very act of pride and self-congratulation and in denying his brotherhood with the person beside him, by his contempt for the tax-gatherer.

Jesus is not saying that God refused to forgive the Pharisee, but that the Pharisee was himself blocking that love and forgiveness by his own pride and dishonesty. His own blindness and dishonesty was blocking the very channel of life which he needed.

Convinced of his own righteousness, the Pharisee in reality went away still locked into his own sinfulness.

Meanwhile, says Jesus, the tax-gatherer who was only too painfully aware of his own faults, simply begged God for mercy. Staring the reality of his failings in the face, he dare not even raise his eyes to heaven. He did not, and in all honesty could not, promise never to sin again. Who could make such a promise anyway?

But, says Jesus, sinner though he was in the eyes of the law, he went away forgiven by God. The one who had so obviously failed to live a good and law-abiding life found in his failure the opportunity for God's love.

The Pharisee believed God's love was a reward: Jesus is saying that it is a gift.

The tax-gatherer would sin again as we all do – and it would be real sin. But Jesus seems to be saying that forgiveness and life are about a relationship of openness and honesty with God, not about being perfect. That is difficult for many of us to take on board, as we know from our own experience. How many times have we heard people ridiculed for confessing their sins to God in church one day – and then going out and sinning the next?

But why do we wash each day when we know we shall inevitably get dirty again? The answer is because we desire to be clean – that is our intent. And we know that, no matter how dirty we may get, we will try to move back to that desired condition. The desire, not the achievement, is what matters.

Nevertheless, it is little wonder if this short and abrasive parable caused enormous anger among the people listening to Jesus. It challenged them in many different areas of their lives.

It is not surprising that Luke describes this story as being 'aimed at' the religious establishment: they believed that prosperity and success were signs of God's blessing – rewards for holy behaviour.

The tragedy was that the poverty and failure so often despised by the religious élite as a sign of God's disapproval, could in reality be the vehicle for his love.

But how in this parable does poverty and failure present the opportunity for life? Where in this story does the Pharisee have offered to him the chance to live? Where is the good news being proclaimed to him?

The Pharisee stands up and makes his arrogant speech to God. But what happens next? Does he walk out of the Temple or does he hear what the tax-gatherer says? Moments after he sits down, he has the chance to hear the honest prayer of someone in touch with the reality of God.

In hearing the words of the tax-gatherer, he is being challenged and given the chance to admit his own self-deceit. How often do we wish that God would give us a clue? That he would quietly whisper in our ear what he wants of us? Instead of which, our faith often seems like a game of blind man's buff as we stumble along trying to make sense of it all.

Maybe that is exactly what was happening to the Pharisee. By admitting his sins before God so frankly, the tax-gatherer was not only in a situation of being able to receive forgiveness himself but, unknowingly, to offer the Pharisee the opportunity for forgiveness also.

Though he refused to acknowledge it, the Pharisee was

hearing a voice which offered him the possibility of life. The good news, though unheard, was being spoken by one of life's self-confessed failures.

But then, as now, no one was listening.

7
Good News From the Poor

In a religious culture which has allowed us to assume that the Gospel is good news for the rich, or at least the educated middle class, it takes a considerable effort of will to think of the good news as being for the poor. We are so conditioned by our inherited model of religion that we instinctively think of the Gospel, if we think of it at all, as being for the churchgoer: which often means the respectable and the well behaved.

As an act of generosity, we may be able to accept that the good news may also be for the poor. But to think that the Gospel is primarily or even solely good news for the poor is difficult for most western Christians.

But if we read the gospels and listen to what this Christ person is saying and doing, then we may have to admit that for him at least the good news had its focus among the poor. And if for him, why not for us also?

What emerges from our reading of the gospels and our encounter with this Christ person, however, is that while the good news may be for the poor, it is not doled out to them like a skid row soup kitchen dishing out hot food.

The Gospel is lived out not *to* the poor but *with* the poor, as proclamation and celebration. This Christ person ate and drank with the poor; he enjoyed their company. They were his friends and his family – his loved ones. And love is a two-way street.

Thus the gospel accounts of Jesus begin to reveal to us a different and even more unsettling idea: that the Gospel may not only be good news for the poor but, as we have begun to suspect, it may also be good news from the poor. This does not mean the poor are some sort of new religious group in disguise, or that they have secretly been studying theology by correspondence course. They are not all suddenly reformed characters. But through them, imperfect though they may be, God often chooses to show his creative love for the world.

Do we really see this happening in the gospels? Perhaps we have already seen this being revealed. The leper is not just healed by Jesus but is touched by the Christ person who thereby shares his defilement. In that touch we see God reaching out and giving life to the most despised and outcast of people. But the leper, by his outrageous act of faith gives us, too, the confidence to ask for life; and by being given life himself he gives us the hope that we too will live. He brings us the good news that the promise and gift can be for us also, no matter who we are.

The woman with the haemorrhage brings us a glimpse of the intended reality of life – despite the injustices of sexual and economic discrimination. If she had not had the courage to reach out and touch the robe of the Christ, she would not have been healed. Jairus would not have passed through a living death into a new and deeper life, and she would not have been the channel of a clear declaration of God's intent for women.

And it is not just a matter of the poor who are poor through no fault of their own, or the sick who are innocent victims of disease: the prodigal son is a powerful symbol that even when we are guilty of stupidity, greed and culpable selfishness the good news can still be there.

The father watched anxiously and in hope for a glimpse of the beloved child, no matter how sinful or unclean that child might be. Disconcertingly, the good news is proclaimed from the sinful child and not from the well-behaved elder brother. Like the sinner in the Temple, the failure of the younger actually created the opportunity for the elder, like the Pharisee, to hear the word of life and come in from the cold.

The gospels show the poor and the outcast not only being accepted, loved and respected, but being involved in the creative process of God: involved in reality and in life. And not only involved, but given a crucial role in that awesome process.

People who have been consigned to a living hell on earth are not simply made well but are able to engage in the process of showing reality to the world which had condemned them: literally bringing the good news of God to other people.

Two figures among many appear in the gospels in ways which may bear this out. Of the first we catch only a fleeting glimpse as he passes out of our sight, but the second is a central figure in the gospel accounts.

THE WILD MAN

The first is a man called Legion (Mark 5.2–20). He has been given that strange name because he is so emotionally or mentally disturbed that it is as though he is possessed by a whole legion of evil spirits. He lives naked and alone among the tombs in a desolate land, caught up in terrible outbursts of violence and rage. He is chained up to protect himself and others but often he breaks the chains and runs wild in a nightmare world of self-destructive madness.

One day he encounters Jesus. The outcome is that the man is calmed and apparently healed. The people from the nearby villages hear what has happened and venture into this wild and desolate place to see for themselves. There, Mark says, they find the man sitting, clothed and in his right mind.

But the good news of healing and life is not only for the one who has been so poor that he has lived naked among the dead in a hell of insanity. Mark insists on continuing the narrative: he says that the man asks to go with Jesus but instead Jesus sends him back into his own community: to tell the people there what God has done.

But Mark says that instead of doing this the man goes away and spreads the news in ten gentile towns and the people are amazed. He goes out from the place of death to spread the good news of God among the gentiles.

The man who has been dead becomes, if we are to believe Mark's account, the first apostle to the gentile world.

OUT OF THE SHADOWS

The other strange figure is that of Mary of Magdala or Mary Magdalene. She too is traditionally believed to have suffered from a mental or emotional illness and to have been healed. A different tradition holds that she had been a prostitute. In either case she would have been an outcast.

There are repeated references to her as one of the companions of Jesus on his travelling ministry but the facts of her life are vague and shadowy: until suddenly she comes into amazingly sharp focus at a crucial point in all four gospels.

All of the gospels carry the account of the execution of Jesus and the burial of his body. The accounts describe a situation of enormous trauma and grief for the friends and followers of Jesus. The one whom they had believed was in some way to bring in the rule of God's sovereign power has been arrested, beaten senseless in a mock trial, stripped naked and put to death like a common criminal. Suddenly it is all over.

But the fact that the gospels were ever written stems from an event which it is claimed occurred after the burial. Whatever it means and whatever happened, the followers of this Christ person were suddenly transformed from being a scattered group of traumatized peasants into a coherent, articulate group of people all claiming the impossible: that the person who had been put to death was alive, and in a powerful and new way.

We are not concerned here to debate the historical facts of what the Church calls the Resurrection. What interests us at this point is who the early Church (in a male-dominated society in which a woman's voice was not even admissible as evidence in court) – who the early church says was the first to discover and to pass on this good news.

Matthew claims that 'Mary of Magdala and the other Mary' are told what has happened and are told to pass the news on to the disciples. Mark says 'Mary of Magdala, Mary the mother of James and Salome' risk their lives to go and anoint the dead body of Jesus. But when they reach the tomb they find the body gone. Instead, they encounter a mysterious figure who tells them to 'give this message to his disciples and Peter . . .'

Luke's account follows the same pattern, ending with the words: 'The women were Mary of Magdala, Joanna, and Mary the mother of James, and they, with the other women told the apostles.' Then, ironically, Luke adds: 'But the story appeared to them to be nonsense, and they would not believe them' (Luke 24.10–11).

John, in his extended account of the event, even describes Mary of Magdala going to the tomb alone and encountering Jesus. And John shows her of all people as being sent by Jesus himself to tell the disciples (John 20.2–18).

How incredible that at the one point in the gospel narratives when it would seem essential to have solid, credible witnesses – and in their culture that would presumably mean men – all four gospel accounts record that the key witnesses to the resurrection were all women. And the first named in all four accounts was this woman from nowhere – Mary of Magdala.

A woman who had not only been healed and restored to normal life but who had now, at least in the minds of the gospel writers and the Christian communities on whose behalf they spoke; become the first to give the good news to the world. Mary of Magdala is the carrier of the absolutely key statement of Good News.

Others also claimed to have received the news and encountered the Christ person, but the first person allowed this discovery was not the inner core of male disciples but Mary of Magdala. Good news from the poor.

If we begin to focus on this possibility of the good news of God's life-giving love being characteristically expressed through the poor, we suddenly see other events in a new way.

Thinking back through the long and troubled history of the community in which Jesus lived, what was the primary event for those people? What was the one encounter with God that seemed to be the reference point of reality for those people? What was it that they believed was the defining moment which spoke to them of the reality of God: of what was real for them?

That primary event was the Exodus. The event by which the community, which had been captured and taken into slavery in Egypt, was delivered and led out into new life. The Exodus was the event by which God created that community out of nothing. God took a people who owned nothing but a few sheep, who were suffering crushing failure and gifted them with promise and life.

The primal event for that people, the people of Jesus the Christ, was God's creative love and mercy. And that love came into play at the time that they were at their weakest. The greatest creative act for that community was articulated through and despite their failure.

Centuries later the former Pharisee, St Paul, was to discover and celebrate the fact that it was when he was weak that the power of God shone through in his life.

The Church has traditionally placed great emphasis on the fact that Paul recognized that God seemed to work through him despite his weakness. But there is another aspect of Paul's life which is even more interesting to us. Whether or not God worked through him when he felt at his weakest, it was actually at the time when Paul was living a life of total cruelty and wickedness that God acted most dramatically.

Whether Mary of Magdala had been a victim of mental illness or whether she had been a prostitute will never be clear. But what seems to be beyond any doubt is that Paul at the time of his 'conversion' or encounter with the Christ was a profoundly evil person. One might almost say a murderer.

It was he who worked with such passion and hatred to root out the followers of Jesus and have them arrested. It was he who was guilty of complicity in the execution of people like the first martyr, Stephen. Paul acted with a relentless violence against the first Christians. Hence the incredulity and alarm of Ananias, the man sent to talk to Paul after his conversion. 'Do you not know the evil this man has done?' he asks in horror.

The good news may come from Paul in many ways but the primary and most overlooked way was that it was while he was still obsessed with his evil persecution of the first Christians that he was called by God to be a channel of the Good News.

The suggestion that reality may be associated with the good news of God, and that this good news may be not only for the poor but from the poor, becomes increasing unpalatable as we explore who in real life these 'poor' actually were: and to whom they were speaking this so-called good news.

Let us remind ourselves what this good news is supposed to mean: if it means anything it means the reality of life – that which gives people meaning and life in real situations. The good news, the life-giving love of God, can be expressed in words; or it can be expressed in giving a thirsty person a cup of water; or in an economic policy decision by the World Bank.

We live in a real world and have the need of real life: of love, security, affirmation, meaning. But how can these fine and noble things be mediated by the poor, the unwashed, the disturbed, and even those classed as evil?

There is one event, poorly documented in the gospels, which nevertheless may speak an outrageously irreverent word of hope and guidance in this dilemma.

It is a single fragment of speech reported in only one gospel: Luke.

It is contradicted by two other writers, Mark and Matthew, and is not even mentioned by John. Why then is it in Luke? Did he make it up or did he speak to witnesses the other writers had not questioned?

8
The Dying Christ

THE FRAGMENT COMES at the most horrific moment for the followers of Jesus: the crucifixion. Finally and inevitably Jesus has been arrested, put on trial, and then made to carry the heavy cross-beam of the gallows on which he is to die.

He is stripped, and nailed to a wooden cross. Crucifixion is not a Jewish custom, it is a brutal form of execution favoured by the occupying Roman armies to make an example of the worst criminals. It is they who are carrying out this execution.

Like thousands before him, Jesus is left hanging naked on the cross to die. Alongside him hang two other criminals whose crimes have been so serious that they too are being executed.

The three men hanging side by side on the gallows are the poorest people in the world. They have been stripped of their possessions, clothing, dignity, hope – and now, finally, their lives.

The horror and suffering of the cross is unspeakably real. Jesus the Christ person is at his most vulnerable and weak: nailed to a filthy cross.

Yet, as Bishop Peter Ball has asked: when was Jesus most completely and effectively living out the love of God? What was the moment when he was most powerfully sharing the Good News?

When do we see God so unconditionally reconciling the world to himself, and making love, the essence of life, real? In that very moment of death. The cross is good news from the poor as the good news had never been before.

How ironic that this profound insight was spoken by a

bishop who was to be forced to resign over a scandal. A vital insight into the good news of God spoken by the one bishop condemned as an unforgivable failure, in the eyes of the religious hierarchy of our own day.

But we are still not at the heart of the matter for Luke. We have still not picked up the vital fragment of evidence. It comes now:

In that agonizing moment of suffering and death on the cross, the whole life and meaning of Jesus appears to have collapsed in ruins. His followers have deserted, denied or betrayed him and he is staring into the face of death. Only two common criminals hang there with him – and they count for nothing.

According to Matthew and Mark Jesus cries out: 'My God, my God why have you forsaken me?'

One of the criminals being executed turns and hurls abuse at Jesus, as do the crowd standing staring up at them.

But, as we know, the other criminal rebukes him and says: 'We deserve our punishment, but this man has not done any wrong.'

Then in this crucial fragment of history, Luke (23.42–3) describes something amazing.

The criminal turns to the Christ person and says: 'Jesus, remember me when you come into your kingdom.'

Time seems to stand still. Did he really say that? Did he actually say 'when' you come into your kingdom; not 'if' you come into your kingdom?

Are we playing games with the most sacred event in the whole of our faith, or is something vital and real happening here?

Can it be, at this point of absolute poverty, weakness and despair, that the word of life is spoken to the dying Son of God? The good news of God's love spoken by an evil, convicted criminal to the Christ?

He calls Jesus by name: he is recognized as a person. 'You are the Christ', he says. 'You will come into your kingdom. And when you do, will you remember me?'

And in that moment of death, when all is lost and he has failed and there is nothing left, it may be that this word of life from the poor brings forth from the lips of the dying Christ the moment of true resurrection: 'You will be with me . . .' he says.

In all the filth and pain, in all the hatred and blood, a common criminal designated by the mighty Roman Empire as an absolute and total failure is the one who ministers the word of life to the Son of God.

Jesus is allowed to die hearing on the lips of a total failure the only words of resurrection life that he was to hear.

But can this be reality? Why did Luke include this small fragment? Did the criminal mean to say what he said? There is no way of knowing. But we can ask the question: would that not be true to the emerging theme in the gospels of the good news being spoken by and from the poor?

The first steps that Jesus took towards the cross were the steps to touch the leper and to sit at table to eat with sinners. Maybe the first hint of resurrection was in the moment when an unrepentant criminal spoke the word of life to the dying Christ.

The whisper of God from the poor?

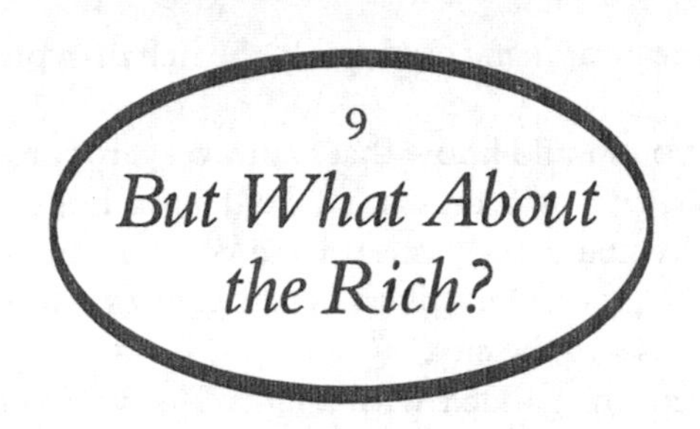

9 But What About the Rich?

THERE WAS ONCE a man who was incredibly rich. He lived in a house made of white marble and surrounded by vast lawns, trees and a large lake. The gates at the end of the long drive were made of wrought iron and were always kept shut.

In addition to the house the man owned two gold Rolls-Royces, ten oil tankers, twenty large factories, and a hundred houses in a big city which he let out at high rents.

Only one thing made the rich man unhappy. At the gates of his fine house sat a poor man. His clothes were in tatters and he walked with an old stick. In fact this stick was the only thing the poor man owned. Each day the poor man came and sat at the gates of the great house. And each day the rich man flew into a terrible rage and ordered his butler to chase him away.

The butler, who hated having to walk down the long drive every day, always gave the poor man a sound thrashing to vent his own anger. But the next day he would always be back.

Then, one day something surprising happened: the rich man and the poor man both died. And because they had died at the very same moment, they found themselves standing together at the gates of heaven.

Except there were no gates: just a broad, slow-moving river with wide flat stepping-stones. And an angel.

'Good morning,' said the angel. 'Welcome to heaven. Before you go in, I need to take down a few details. Who are you both?'

Before the poor man could speak, the rich man pushed forward.

'I think you should know that I am a very important man,' he said. 'When I was on earth I built up a huge industrial empire. I owned a big house made of white marble, two gold Rolls-Royces, ten oil tankers, twenty factories, and a hundred houses in the city.'

He paused, then added with a sigh: 'But you know what they say: you can't take it with you when you go.'

The angel looked surprised: 'You can't take it with you? Oh, but you can. In fact we insist. You bring with you all that you have owned. The only snag is that we haven't yet built a bridge, so I'm afraid you have to carry your own luggage. But it's not far: you just go across those flat stepping-stones and all of heaven is open before you.'

The angel turned to the poor man: 'You shouldn't have any trouble. The only luggage you have is your stick. Take your time: there's no hurry.'

Steadying himself with his stick, the poor man walked slowly and carefully across the wide flat stepping-stones into heaven. And in the distance there was the sound of music and laughter.

But by now the rich man was very angry. 'Do you mean to say I have to carry everything I own across those stepping-stones?' he shouted. 'Do you realize how much property I own? It will take forever to carry all my possessions across that river.'

There was a moment of complete silence. The distant music and laughter was hushed.

'Yes,' said the angel. 'I think you may be right.'

Behind Gold Bars

Faced with massive and often unnecessary suffering in the world it is easy to cast the rich in the role of evil oppressor.

And it has to be said that most people who are rich did not arrive at that point by chance: they became rich because they wanted to be rich and fought to be rich even when other people suffered in that process. And having become rich, people often wish to remain rich. They support political and economic systems that protect their wealth.

But in a way the rich are trapped by their wealth and possessions almost as much as the poor are trapped by their poverty. During the long years of apartheid in South Africa, it was difficult for many people to have any sympathy with the wealthy, white population whose policies oppressed and dehumanized the black population. It was hard to see that in dehumanizing the black people, the whites were also dehumanizing themselves.

In a world of tabloid communication, and increasingly tabloid religion, it is easy to fall into the trap of categorizing people as good and evil. It is easy to give people a label, and not to honestly ask who they are and why they are like that. It is an easy way of avoiding real encounter and real relationship.

Given his love for the poor, and his determination to always show them in particular the openness of God, we might have expected to see the Christ person condemning the rich out of hand.

And he does condemn some people: or at least tells them they have condemned themselves. But they are characteristically people blinded by pride and arrogance – and by the false righteousness of religious custom.

But the people who are materially wealthy seem to be treated in a rather surprising way by someone who was so supportive of the poor. But always Jesus seems to point us to the question we began with: what is real? What is really happening?

A series of incidents gives us a clue as to what that reality may be. And they are incidents from real life.

RISKING EVERYTHING

In the first incident (Luke 20.45—21.4), Jesus and his followers are at the great Temple in Jerusalem. There they see important people called doctors of the law who love to walk up and down in their fine robes; they always take the best seats at public events and sit in the places of honour at great feasts.

But the reality, says Jesus, is that they swindle widows out of their savings and say long prayers in public just to impress other people.

As Jesus and his friends watch, they see rich people coming and putting large sums of money into the Temple treasury. They are probably being generous and sincere in their giving to God. But then comes a poor widow who puts just two tiny copper coins into the treasury. As she does this Jesus says something about reality: she has put into the treasury more than they have, he says. They have given of their wealth, with no risk of discomfort or insecurity, while she, who has less than enough to live on, has given everything she has in the world. Now she has nothing to live on: she has offered God her life.

Jesus does not condemn the rich but he does point to the reality of the situation: and the core of that reality is relationship.

THE MAN UP THE TREE

The second incident is both important and humorous. It comes a few pages earlier in Luke (19.2–10), and is the story about a rich and unpopular man who was not very tall. His name was Zacchaeus and he was hated by the people because he collected taxes for the Roman army of occupation. Not only did he collect the money, he was suspected of syphoning off large amounts in unofficial commission for himself. He worked for the enemy and robbed his own people at the same time. This is Luke's story:

One day Jesus comes to the town where Zacchaeus lives. Zacchaeus, who is curious to see what all the fuss is about, goes out into the street to catch sight of this Christ person. The problem is, as in so many gospel accounts, the outsider cannot get near to Jesus because of all his followers. Instead,

Zacchaeus is confronted by a wall of people all much taller than him and all with their backs to him.

Zacchaeus, who is determined to see the controversial visitor, has an idea. He runs down the road ahead of the crowd and climbs a tree. But as Jesus and the crowd are walking past, Jesus stops and calls out to him. 'Come down from the tree,' he says. And then adds to everyone's surprise: 'I must come and stay with you today.'

Again we are plunged back into the scandal of the fellowship meals of Jesus, and sure enough, the religious authorities are on hand to condemn him: he has gone in to be the guest of a sinner, they say.

But something has happened to Zacchaeus. During the meal he suddenly stands up and makes an announcement: 'Here and now I give half my possessions to charity and if I have cheated anyone I will repay them four times over.'

If Jesus had laughed at the sight of the superintendent of taxes perched half-way up a sycamore tree, he must have smiled with delight at the speech that his host has just made. Giving half his possessions to charity would help a large number of poor people, but that is not the reality that Jesus is looking at. Something more has happened which prompts Jesus to exclaim with delight: 'Salvation has come to this house today!'

What is salvation? Salvation is about life, and life is a core element of reality as we experience it. No matter how much we may argue about the meaning of the word reality the most important fact about what is real is that we are alive.

But how has life and 'reality' come to this rich man? He has not in any way bought life by his generous gesture but he has suddenly been liberated from his addiction to money and power. Zacchaeus has been so hooked on money that he has been willing to betray his own people for it, and to earn their hatred so that he can have more and more of it

Letting go of a huge amount of that money is a sign that he has been freed from his addiction. Like Scrooge in *A Christ-*

mas Carol he is freed to live and to discover a reality he had formerly denied.

He does not give all his money away. But by the willingness of Jesus to come into his house and share food, and to risk his reputation in order to befriend him, a barrier and an isolation has been broken. He has been set free. His decision to give his money away is not payment but celebration. His wealth, to most people a sign of success, has in reality been masking failure. The possession which most people desire has been his prison.

TRAPPED BY WEALTH

The same reality we see revealed in Luke's story of Zacchaeus is also explored in a story in Mark's gospel (10.17–22). In fact Mark sets two incidents side by side in order to make absolutely clear the reality he wants us to grasp.

As Jesus starts out on a journey, a stranger suddenly runs up and kneels before him: 'Good master,' he says, 'what must I do to win eternal life?' There is a gentle humour in Mark's story. The young man who is very rich has rushed, full of passion and urgency, to ask Jesus the most important question in the world: how can I really live? But Jesus teases him.

'Why do you call me good?' he asks the young man. 'Only God is good.' But this is not just teasing; Jesus is also saying something profound about reality and about God.

Jesus continues the exchange. 'You know the law', he says to the young man. 'Isn't that the way to eternal life?'

In exasperation the young man says: 'But I have obeyed the law ever since I was a boy.' The clear inference is that the law has been honestly tried and found wanting. The young man is honest enough to acknowledge this and still be passionately seeking after reality.

But in that exchange the mood of the encounter changes. The gentle teasing stops and Jesus faces the young man with a stark choice. The choice is between life and death. 'One thing you lack; one thing hinders you', Jesus says. 'Go and sell all that you possess and give the money to the poor and follow me, and you will have life.'

Suddenly, the rich young man is faced with an impossible decision. All his security is tied up in his wealth. All that he is has been defined by his wealth. He was very rich.

He makes his decision: he walks away.

But within that brief encounter which may only have taken a few moments, Mark tells us that something else happens. Something vitally important.

The rich young man is saying to Jesus: I have obeyed all the law but still it is not the answer.

There, at that moment when the teasing stops, Mark says Jesus loved him. The words actually mean that Jesus embraced him. In the middle of this story, Jesus is so moved by the tragedy of this poor boy trapped in his wealth that he puts his arm round him and hugs him.

Why does Mark bother to report such a trivial detail and what does it matter? Perhaps it matters hugely. It demonstrates that the attitude of Jesus was one of love, compassion and encouragement: not one of outright condemnation and dismissal. He does not send the rich young man away, he tells him: I love you.

It is the rich young man who pulls away, and chooses to take his wealth with him on the road which he knows will not lead him to life.

Why did Jesus tell him to give his money to the poor? Not because he was at that moment trying to change the condition of the poor, but because he was simply concerned to give the rich young man what he was asking for: reality, and life.

He was saying that the riches the young man possessed acted as a barrier to life, a barrier to an engagement with reality: a barrier to a right relationship with God – one of trust – and a right relationship with his neighbour in the form of justice for the poor.

But, unlike Zacchaeus, the rich young man could not let go of his material wealth, even though it was that wealth which in reality was consigning him to death. Sadly he walks away from the Christ person – and no doubt Jesus was grieved to see him go.

AN ACT OF COURAGE

But Mark is not content to leave the matter there. Only a few lines later in his narrative he tells us a second story which is the mirror image of the rich young man. It is the story of Bartimaeus, the blind beggar (Mark 10.46–52).

As ever, Jesus is on a journey. As he walks along the road he is followed and surrounded by a large crowd. They are his disciples and other people intent on hearing what he is saying.

Sitting in the dust at the roadside is a blind beggar, Bartimaeus. He hears the crowd approaching and he asks what is happening. When he is told it is Jesus he shouts out: 'Son of David, Jesus, have pity on me.'

The words he uses are important – but so is what happens next.

The crowd, typically, tell the lowly beggar to stop shouting and making a fuss: they are trying to listen to the words of this holy teacher.

But Bartimaeus shouts all the louder. 'Son of David, have pity on me.'

Jesus hears him shouting and stops. He asks the disciples to call him and the blind man leaps to his feet, pushing through the disapproving crowd to get to Jesus.

'What do you want me to do for you?' asks Jesus. As with the rich young man, Jesus assumes nothing and imposes nothing on the stranger. He simply asks the vital question: what is it that you are asking for?

Unable to see Jesus, Bartimaeus says: 'I want my sight back again.' Once he was able to see, but now he is blind.

Jesus heals him with the words: 'Go, your faith has healed you.' But the blind man, who has been given the freedom of sight and the freedom to go and live his life among his own people, stays and follows this Christ person down the road.

* * *

The comparison with the story of the rich young man is obvious. The rich man who could see, was blind to the reality of life; but the blind man who was living in bitter poverty could somehow see the reality of who Jesus was. The words 'Son of David' which Mark says he used, were the well-known title for the Messiah, the chosen one of God. In his blindness and from the gutter, the words of affirmation and acknowledgement are spoken to Jesus by the poor.

But as with the story of the rich young man, Mark describes a vital clue which is usually overlooked or regarded as unimportant. Let us run the film again – but slowly this time. What is the clue, Watson?

The beggar is sitting at the roadside. Unable to see, he can only know what is happening by sound and touch. Unable to work, his life is a constant struggle for survival. Occasionally, people throw a small coin down to him as he sits in the dust. Unable to see the coin and to prevent it getting lost among the passing feet, he spreads his cloak before him to catch the precious coins. At night he hides himself away, finding shelter where he can and wrapping himself in his cloak against the cold.

The only thing in the world that he possesses is the cloak. It is vitally important to him as he begs for money by day, and it is the one friend and protector that keeps him alive by night. The cloak is his life.

But what does Mark say? What are the words that are lost in the middle of this dramatic story?

The blind man shouts out to Jesus above the murmurings of the crowd, and Jesus calls him. In exultation and joy the blind beggar leaps to his feet and throws off his cloak in his haste to get to Jesus.

He throws off the cloak which has suddenly become a hindrance, a barrier between him and Jesus. But Bartimaeus is still blind. In the darkness he does not know where the cloak has gone or whether someone has stolen it. He does not know whether he will ever find it again.

He throws aside his one possession and his source of life

and protection. He is, in that moment, totally committed to this Christ person whom he has never seen and who, at that point, has not even spoken a word to him.

People who are homeless in Britain today tend to guard their meagre possessions well. Years ago, homeless men staying in the grim old hostel dormitories would sleep in their coats for fear of having them stolen. Some who have lived that life for years will continue to sleep in their coats today, even after being rehoused in warm modern accommodation with secure individual rooms.

Homeless people who are often labelled as beggars live on the edge of life and death. They see their friends die from cold. They do not part readily with the things that keep them alive: their coats and their shoes.

The cloak is crucial in Mark's story – as crucial as the wealth of the rich young man, and the two copper coins given by the poor widow at the Temple.

It is crucial because it signals to us the reality that Mark, from the first words of his urgent, passionate, crude and fragmentary gospel, is trying to reveal to us.

The reality is one of relationship.

What was the poor widow's relationship with God? What was the rich young man's relationship with God? What was blind Bartimaeus' relationship with God? All of them believed that God constituted the core of reality for them. But they had different ways of responding to that reality.

The poor widow and the blind beggar entered into that relationship with a trust that endangered their own lives: they put everything on the line. But the rich young man who obeyed all the religious rules could not make that leap of faith: even when he had been held in the arms of the one person who Mark believed embodied that reality.

10
And What About Us?

TUMBLING THROUGH THE gospels in pursuit of Mark and Luke we encounter a hundred people who, like Bartimaeus, have met this Christ person. Whether rich young men, or blind old men, lepers or madmen, they all met and heard and were touched by this person.

But what about us: how can we have an encounter that could even begin to resemble a relationship? How, in any sense of the word can we 'meet' this person? A person who never wrote down a single thought and about whom we have only a patchwork of knowledge and evidence.

Is it not better to turn away, either in sadness or relief, and put all this behind us? If we cannot meet and explore, and test out and know, then what does it matter anyway?

Can we know? Or is the concept of such an encounter so ridiculous to our modern minds that we will not entertain it – far less trust it? Will we, like the rich young man, turn away?

Or dare we step forward, and risk confronting that possibility – which most intelligent people dismiss as fantasy? It is a risk that takes enormous courage; a risk that blind Bartimaeus took, not once but twice.

The first moment of risk was, as we have seen, when he leapt to his feet and threw aside his cloak in his haste to get to the Christ person. The second moment of risk was when Jesus asked him the seemingly pointless question: 'What do you want me to do for you?'

But the question was not pointless. It was not at all obvious that the blind man would want his sight back: he might more sensibly have realized that this was a rational impossibility, and asked instead for a blessing from Jesus or strength to bear his disability – or even simply money on which to live.

Further, faced with the real possibility of receiving his sight, Bartimaeus might well have shrunk back from the frightening new responsibilities that life as a sighted person would bring. Sometimes when we are faced with the possibility of healing, we realize that we have found a strange security in the pain of weakness and failure. We hesitate to throw away the crutches which have been our support and excused us from so much that challenges us in life. We do not always want to risk the uncertainties of our new-found freedom.

The failures of the past can become an excuse for not living the future.

Bartimaeus may have felt he was too set in his ways or too old to change, and opted for less than the gift of life that in his darkness he sensed he was being offered. But then, freely and of his own choice, Bartimaeus takes the colossal risk of faith by asking the Christ person for his sight.

That event took place two thousand years ago, but it may have something important to say to us today. Like Bartimaeus, it may be that we too are seeking for life. But unlike him we may be afraid to ask for the thing we desire most. Perhaps we are uneasy about the possible consequences of such a request being granted.

And in any case, who would we ask? It is one thing to ask a doctor to be made well, but it is quite another to ask anyone for the gift of knowing that we are truly alive.

And who would be able to give us an answer? Intellectuals, politicians or philosophers? Or would we have the courage and the foolishness to ask the person that Bartimaeus asked?

To stand in the dark and to ask that person for life is at the heart of something we have not yet considered: prayer. And perhaps, in our story of contradictions and surprises, the unlikely place called prayer may be where we should explore our relationship with this Christ person and find the key to what is real.

Discovering Prayer

How can the possibility of prayer bring us into any sort of real contact with the Christ person – or with God? To most people, prayer is something strange and unreal that happens in dark and gloomy church buildings but which has nothing to do with real life. How can prayer have anything to do with our search for reality and meaning?

Perhaps before we answer that question we need to think for a moment about what prayer means.

Prayer is either a quaint and meaningless religious custom or it is the most important activity in the history of the universe. Either God is the source of all meaning, all purpose and life; or simply the product of empty, superstitious minds.

If spirituality is about our awareness of God and how we understand our relationship with God, then prayer has to do with the way we live our response to that relationship. Prayer is about relationship. And that relationship is about life.

Imagine a man sitting in a room. Near the window there is a plant in a pot. The man is the higher form of life. He has a brain, eyes, ears, hands and feet. He can think, walk, see and hear. He has intelligence. But he is often confused. He receives conflicting messages. He smokes and drinks things which damage him. He does not know where life comes from. Often he seeks death.

The plant on the window ledge has no eyes or ears; no brain. But it turns its face towards the sun and pushes its roots deep into the soil. Always it seeks life. The plant turns towards the sun but it cannot see the sun. It reaches down into the soil with its roots even though it does not know what moisture is.

Prayer has about it that same sense of turning and seeking life, even though we may not understand or know the meaning of God. It is not about our own knowledge, skill, strength or intelligence or about our ability to speak in some special religious language.

Above all, it is about listening: listening to God.

SOUNDS IN THE SILENCE

Some years ago, there was an explosion deep underground at a coal mine in the United States. Many miners were killed instantly in the blast but a small group was trapped by the roof-fall.

At the pit head no one knew whether anyone was left alive below ground, but immediately a rescue operation was launched in the hope that they would find someone.

Rescue teams went down to the level at which the explosion had occurred. Then began the long and dangerous task of digging through the tons of rock blocking the tunnel. It was a race against time: there would be very little oxygen and, if any miners were left alive, they might be badly injured.

Behind the wall of rock, in the darkness, the small group of trapped miners waited. Each hour was like an eternity, as they lay cold and frightened and in constant fear that they would be crushed to death by a new fall of rock. At first they tried to laugh and joke to keep their spirits up, but as time went on they fell silent and listened. They listened intently for the sound of pickaxes; a sound that would tell them that help was at hand. The sound of life.

Finally they thought they heard a noise. There was silence. Then, faintly and a long way off, they heard the sound of tapping as their rescuers tried to signal to them. Hours later their rescuers broke through: gently and carefully the trapped miners were helped to safety.

They had listened because their lives depended on it. They had listened intently because hearing the sound of their rescuers was more important than anything else. They listened for the sound of life.

Prayer is about listening for the sound of God. We cannot block out the other sounds and signals we receive every minute of the day, but to pray is to listen for God. It is to be attentive to the voice of God, even when there is noise all around us and only silence from God.

If prayer is about relationship and that relationship is one of love, then we listen to God as we listen to someone who loves us. And if we speak, we speak as we would to someone we love. Jesus taught his friends to speak to God with the simplicity and trust that a child would have for a loving parent.

When We Get Stuck

Down the centuries, the Church has created thousands of written prayers and many people find these useful. But we do not have to use these traditional prayers. Often we may find their language and style a hindrance rather than a help. We need to remember that when we pray we are not performing; we are not actors. We are speaking to someone who cares deeply for us and who is holding us in their love.

We are very sensibly told that when we pray we should say thank you for all the good things we enjoy in life; we should say we are sorry for all the damaging things we have done to other people – and the good things we have failed to do; we should ask God to be with people who are in trouble and sickness and despair so they know they are not alone; and we should tell God that we love him.

But still people say they find it very difficult to pray: they do not know the right words; they don't feel anything; and they are sure that nothing is happening. What they mean is they find it hard to pray in the way they think they should pray, and with the results they think they should achieve.

But the praying is more in the wanting to pray than the words we use. The trying to pray is more important than the complexity of our language. We do not love someone because they are clever with words; in fact it is often easier to love someone who is not at all clever, with words or with anything else.

Imagine a small child painting a picture at school. At the

end of the day they bring the painting home to show their mother. But walking home their picture gets dropped onto the muddy path. When the child finally arrives breathless at the house to present their painting it is creased, smudged and muddy. The child has not deliberately spoiled the painting: it's just what happens on the way home from school on a rainy day when you are five years old and in a hurry.

But does the mother reject the gift because it is not perfect? Does she not love both the painting and the smudges? And is it not more precious to her than a Rembrandt or a Picasso? The love is in the giving, not the gift. Our love is in the praying, not the prayer.

What Happens When We Pray?

Some people believe that God answers prayer in a direct cause-and-effect way. Rather like putting a coin in a slot machine and immediately getting a bar of chocolate out. Other people do not accept this theory: they believe that God hears our prayer but that the result is not always, if ever, clear. And if there is an answer, it is frequently: no.

But perhaps a more helpful way to think of prayer is again in terms of a relationship with God and with other people. If we think along these lines then, two things seem to happen when we pray.

First: prayer reduces distance.

When the little boy who had cancer was in hospital, hundreds of people began praying for him in the village where he lived. As they thought and prayed about him and his mother they were brought closer to them. They had all lived in the same village for years, but most would not have been able to say what the little boy or his mother looked like.

But as they prayed for them, they pictured them in their mind's eye; they thought about the pain they were suffering, and began to feel a tiny part of that pain themselves. They shared the hope and the anxiety; they talked with their neighbours about how things were going. It was real and immediate to them.

Gradually, the whole community became focused on the little boy in hospital and it was decided to raise some money to send him and his family on a holiday to America. People who hardly knew each other ganged together to organize a sponsored parachute jump. What was happening miles away in a big city hospital became increasingly part of their own lives. The distance between them and the child was reduced.

Miles away in hospital, he was closer to them than when he was fit and well and living unnoticed in the next street.

Second: prayer changes people.

Prayer may not change the weather; the outcome of a lottery draw; or find us a parking space when we so urgently need one; but prayer does seem to change people.

When we truly pray for someone, we are loving them. We are willing what is best for them, whether it is guidance or healing. As we pray for them we begin to appreciate them more as a person, as well as reflecting on their situation, their needs and problems. As we hold the person before God we are reminded that God not only loves them deeply and unconditionally, but that God loves us too.

Both we and the person we are praying for are being loved by God. We see that we are held in a common bond of caring, love and respect. And that sharing of love is a life-giving process in which people change and grow.

But real life is not always sweetness and light. In one of his hardest sayings, we are told that Jesus commanded us to love our enemies. Most of us would say that was impossible and reject the idea out of hand.

Jesus was not saying that we should like our enemy, or that we should find it enjoyable to love them. To love, is to will and to work for the well-being of the other person.

But prayer is an event, not a theory; just as love is a social activity, not an ideal. So the question is not how do we think we would feel loving our enemy, or how would we reason that it might be possible or sensible to do so: the real question is what happens when we actually pray for our enemy: someone we hate or dislike intensely?

As we have said, to pray for that person means to place our relationship with them alongside God's relationship with them. At first this is very hard to do: rather like putting two magnets together the wrong way. They repel.

But if we persist with this over a period of time, the realization gradually begins to sink in that while we are struggling to pray for them, God is all the while loving them. And loving us. The other person may not be changed by our prayer, but it is highly likely that we shall be changed. Maybe we shall be healed, and that change in us may have a knock-on effect in people whom we have regarded as our enemy.

Rather like the story of the rich young man, it is as though God has one arm round our 'enemy' and another arm round us. It is a strange experience which often, if not always, produces surprising results.

11
Getting Angry With God

PRAYER MAY BE about listening, but it is also about being honest. Sometimes uncomfortably honest. The problem with praying for our enemies is that it demands that we try to be honest about our relationships with other people. We have to be honest when we pray, because prayer is relationship and no relationship can work unless we speak the truth. That is why many of us refuse to pray for people we dislike: we pretend we cannot pray for them.

The trouble is, we get too polite about prayer. People who go to church are usually polite to each other, at least on the surface, and so we assume that Jesus was also polite, and therefore that we have be polite to him and to God.

But polite in that sense usually means a lack of honesty: pretending that things are not as they are. That is why people find it difficult to pray when they are angry: with themselves, with each other, or with God. We are brought up to assume we must always be calm and serene in our prayers.

But what sort of real and loving relationship forbids any expression of anger, frustration or pain? What sort of friend or lover says there are things we may never discuss? What sort of friendship is it where one person does not genuinely want to hear how the other person feels?

One of the great things about a real friendship or a loving relationship is that you can open your heart to the other person and be fairly sure you will not be rejected.

There are times when anger, a shout of rage, even obscene abuse hurled at God can truly be prayer. No matter what violent words a person in pain is using they may be saying to God: I hurt and you have let me be hurt.

PRAYERS OF RAGE

Many years ago a young mother died suddenly, leaving her husband to bring up their two small children. She had walked into the house from the car and collapsed without warning. She was dead before the ambulance arrived.

They had been very much in love and the husband had been shattered by the experience. But he had not gone to pieces. He coped well at the funeral. He had, they said, been very brave. The vicar called often, and they talked about how life would be in the future.

Then, in the course of one of these conversations, the flood gates suddenly opened and the man began to sob. Looking up, he shouted at God in an uncontrollable rage: 'You bastard. You bloody bastard.' It was a rage that came from the depths. It was probably the first prayer he had ever uttered. He had stopped being polite to the vicar and started being totally honest with God, with himself and with everyone else.

His wife was not brought back to life and the pain did not suddenly go away. But something had changed. A barrier was broken and the long process of healing had begun.

* * *

It is permitted to be angry with God and to shout at God: and that can be prayer just as much as the serene worship of a cathedral.

There are times when life becomes unbearably painful; there are times when God does seem to be a total bastard; and honesty demands that we pray that pain and that anger. Because if we pretend they don't exist, we damage our relationship with God – and we damage ourselves by suppressing that rage.

And if God cannot take occasional rage, frustration and bad language, then he is not the God of the Christ who shouted in his pain and dying: 'My God, why have you forsaken me?'

The barbed fish-hook needs to go deeper before it can be freed. It may be that we need to acknowledge the pain and anger of the situation before we can be free to find healing. And maybe God knows that.

The Great Darkness

Often there will be times of pain and anger, but occasionally we may find that we have entered the great darkness of depression. There are times when we believe we cannot pray because we cannot find even a word of anger to speak out loud. Sometimes people buried in deep depression are not even able to put a thought together in their minds.

There is only a leaden and cold silence. The feeling that you live in a different world from any other human being: and there is no God. The distance between you and the next human being is an infinity.

Can we pray without a word? When we are in that terrible and lonely place, all our senses tell us that we cannot. But perhaps it is at those times we know we cannot pray, that God is praying for us. Speaking the words of love we cannot hear, and if we could, would not believe. If the one who created us gave us the gift of prayer, then perhaps there are times when God does not need our words or thoughts to know we love in return. Watching at the bed of a sick child the loving parent does not need to be told they are loved.

Even when we are not in such an extreme situation we may find it impossible to pray: to listen and to speak to God with any sense that anything is there. It is a common experience and one in which we may be tempted to give up. Religious people know it well, and wag their heads like old gardeners and say sagely it is a 'dry spell' that may pass.

But in a perverse way, that may be just the time to carry on in prayer: the time when we feel we receive nothing in return may be the one time that prayer is a true gift to God: something offered with no experience or expectation of anything in return.

Does God Speak To Us?

Do we ever get anything in return? Does God ever talk to us?

If we are suggesting that prayer is primarily about listening, then what is it we are listening for? Does the voice of God come booming out of the sky like some cosmic public address system? That may be how some people have described it, but other people believe they hear God speaking in less dramatic ways.

God spoke, and still speaks to us today, through the person of Jesus the Christ. What this Christ person did and said is not only characteristic of God's will, but through him God is speaking to us here and now. God is in some way 'in' this Christ person so that if we speak to this Jesus in our prayers we are addressing God.

Second, God speaks to us through the gospels we have been exploring and through many other parts of the Bible. The documents that make up the Bible were obviously written in a different culture and in vastly different circumstances to those we live in today. So we need to take great care that we do not simply read off the words and situations as if they were written directly to us here and now.

Even so, it is not difficult to believe that many of the things Jesus spoke to his followers also apply to us: that in a sense he might well be saying some of those things to us today. Perhaps above all, if we read the gospels day by day we will find ourselves growing deeper into a relationship with God which gives meaning and purpose to our lives.

Third, God may speak to us through other people. Through our love, our friendships and conversations; through hearing other people's experience of God; through agnostics and even through atheists.

Despite all its failings, the Church has for the past two thousand years been trying to hear and to reflect on God's will and purpose for the world. If we think of the Church not as an institution but as a community of people, we see that many if not most of them are struggling to follow the Christ person in their lives. It may be that we will hear God speaking to us through the shared experience of those people. They may even hear the word of God through us.

Fourth, God may speak to us through the created world. Many people have a sense of awe and wonder when they see the beauty of the world and believe that God is to be encountered in this wonder.

Some would reject this as being completely arbitrary. Whether we regard a sunset as beautiful or not may simply be a subjective view of a physical event. But others would say there is such a thing as beauty and there is such a thing as wonder: and through these experiences we get a glimpse of God. It may be that we see the artist through the painting.

But what's the point?

* * *

If there is no God, then prayer is a meaningless activity which degrades us and makes us less than human. But if there *is* God, and if God is in any way at the core of reality, then prayer is a vital way in which we ourselves become more real. By affirming and engaging in the relationship which God offers we are not being asked to become more religious – but more alive.

If prayer is God's word to us then we need to remember just what God's word means: it is God's word that creates the universe; that forms us in the womb; that calls us to love our neighbour, and our enemy as ourselves. To hear God's word is to hear the life-giving, dynamic challenge to take part in the process of creation.

Just as the word of God is powerful and effective in action, so our prayer cannot be limited to the spoken word. We pray not only our words; we also pray our actions. Our prayer is not just our words in response to God but our lives in response to God.

This breaks down the false division between faith and life;

between God and the world; between our worship and our daily living; between body and soul. It allows the sacred to flood into all of our day to day activities; it begins to recognize the sacred already there.

Suddenly, prayer is not just something that religious people do in churches on Sundays, but something that should happen every day of the week in every aspect of our lives in the world.

So not only is our silent attentiveness to God truly prayer; or the words spoken or thought before God for another person; but our work should be part of our prayer; fighting social injustice is part of our prayer; sex can be part of our prayer; and parenting may be part of our prayer.

If prayer is a crucial way in which we engage with the reality of life, then it seems incomprehensible that we should try to restrict it to a designated and fenced-off area of existence called religion.

Prayer is not a compartmentalized religious activity; it is a life activity: an engagement with reality in its fullness. It does not have the effect of shutting us away but brings us out into the open to discover still more of life.

Prayer is the crucial way in which we make the connection between the powerful, troublesome Word of God embodied in the Christ person of the gospels and our own lives. Prayer may give us a glimpse of the artist through the painting, but as the man with the lettuce discovered, it is not always a pretty picture.

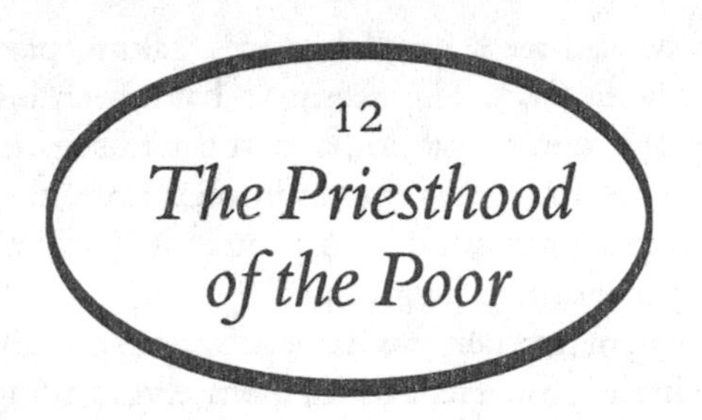

12
The Priesthood of the Poor

IF REALITY IS to be found in the encounter with God through prayer and through a loving relationship with other people, we might expect this discovery to bring a sense of freedom and happiness.

We may feel moved to be more open and generous with our neighbour and to share other people's experience of God. And down the years many people have responded in this way.

But sometimes the reality has been very different. Instead of an outgoing sense of freedom and happiness, a natural instinct for preservation and security seems to have taken over.

What happens when we receive something precious? We want to guard it, to put it in a strongbox, to build walls round it. What we have, we want to keep: to protect and to control. We have something of value and we want to possess it: to make it ours.

We see this happening in our economic and political decision making. The result is that the gap between the rich and the poor grows wider, regardless of the degradation and suffering caused by that division. Those who have possessions are intent on keeping them and adding to them, in ways which are often far beyond any realistic sense of need.

Meanwhile, to keep our investment portfolios attractive and productive, millions of people die from hunger and cold and countless others are denied the most basic human rights: clean air to breathe and clean water to drink.

Is it not the case that we instinctively want to keep what we have and to defend it against any outside threat?

Perhaps we can see a parallel process taking place in our relationship with God. This seems to have been historically true down the ages as we look at the Church. Instead of being a channel for God's unconditional love, the Church has often been a fortress built to protect its faith: as though faith was a possession to be guarded.

And human nature being what it is, we can actually see this happening in the gospel narratives themselves among the followers of Jesus.

BASIC INSTINCT

There is for example, a strange incident which is described in the gospels of Mark, Matthew and Luke, in which Jesus takes his closest disciples up to the top of a mountain. There, say the gospel writers, the appearance of Jesus is changed and his clothes appear to shine with a brilliant light.

The disciples see two other people with Jesus, who are described as Moses the lawgiver, and Elijah – who appears to represent the prophetic tradition of the community. For the moment we are not concerned how this bizarre event might have come about: it is the response of the disciples which is significant for us here.

In a situation of sudden wonder and amazement in which the Christ person is apparently revealed as being the consummation of both the religious law and the prophetic tradition, there is an instinctive reaction.

The response of the disciples is to want to build shelters to house each of the three people. Their instinct is to prolong the experience: to make it permanent. To build walls round it: to preserve it.

But already the experience is at an end, and Jesus is leading them back down the hillside as he begins his final approach to Jerusalem where he is to meet his death.

The disciples may or may not have seen reality on the hilltop but their response, though natural and forgivable, is inappropriate. The Christ event can not become static and fixed or walled in.

But after the strange incident on the hilltop, there follows a further dramatic incident to do with the same issue of preservation and protection. There is an argument between Jesus and one of the disciples, probably Peter. Jesus has tried to warn his followers that his destiny is not to become an earthly king with power and wealth. Instead, he must suffer and die at the hands of the religious authorities.

Horrified, Peter instinctively tries to divert Jesus from this disastrous line of action. In a passionate plea he urges him to turn aside from this collision course with death. But Jesus rounds on Peter and warns him not to hinder or stand in the way of what is bound to happen.

Again, the natural human instinct is to protect what is loved and valued; to keep what has been given, even to the extent of denying its real purpose. But this natural instinct is met with anger by Jesus in a situation which may reveal the depth of his own human fear and sorrow at what is to happen. No matter what the cost, the Christ event cannot be shielded from painful reality.

The Glass Wall

We see a similar process happening with the community of faith which began to form after Christ's death. The first three gospels show Jesus as being open and inclusive in his relationships with other people: controversially the poor, the sinful and the outcast. There were no barriers. As we have seen, it was his deliberate insistence on inclusiveness, and the inference that this was the will and purpose of God, that was one of the causes of his arrest and execution.

But when we come to look at the writings of people like St Paul, we see a significant shift from this unconditional acceptance by Jesus, to a pattern whereby the followers of Christ form a distinct group.

What appears in the life of the Christ person as an indistinct series of overlapping and open relationships and events, now becomes a finite grouping dependent on faith and marked by a rite of initiation. What seems to have begun as unconditional friendship has now started to look uncomfortably like formal membership.

And a parallel process appears to take place in the later writings of John. Even though John insists that God loves the world and that the Christ event is brought about as an expression of that love, there is in John a clear tendency to distinguish between the 'higher' spirit and the 'lower' flesh. But this is hardly characteristic of the person who expressed the reality of God by touching lepers and embracing the defiled.

Again we see the tendency to build a wall: this time a glass wall between the earthly and the spiritual. The wall seems intended to define and protect the priceless gift, but is in great danger of denying its whole meaning and purpose.

This dualistic model of thought: spirit and flesh; higher and lower; light and darkness, is only one step away from the righteous and sinful, clean and unclean distinctions, which were the very barriers the Christ person fought to destroy in the ecclesiastical system of his own day.

* * *

Finally we come to the Eucharist, the central act of worship of most of the western Church, in which the last meal of the Christ person is re-enacted and relived.

This act of worship is normally open only to the formal membership of the church who have undergone a rite of initiation. During the liturgy the assembled group declares itself to be set apart in a special relationship to the Christ person; to the implicit exclusion of all others who are not of that company.

But what was the nature of that last meal of the Christ person? First, it was the meal which he unconditionally shared with the very people who were about to betray, deny and desert him in his hour of greatest need.

Second, this meal so celebrated and reverenced is also a remembering of the fellowship meals which Jesus shared with the failures of this world: the sinful, poor and defiled outcasts of another religious system.

In our attempt to protect the gift, we are in great danger of denying its meaning. But is the reality of God's love so fragile? Or is it our vested interest that we feel is under threat? Can the reality of God be mediated only through our formal religious structures and an ordained priesthood which we can control?

But what is the alternative? If reality is to do with God and if God is to be encountered wherever we meet the Christ person, then where shall we find him?

The Heartbeat of the Gospel

Traditionally, we may look within the great structures of ecclesiastical power to encounter the Christ person. And we may find him there. But two thousand years ago we encounter him among the poor: sharing their love and their suffering.

Is it completely impossible that we shall find him there today? May we not encounter the Christ person living out the love of God in our own world, in places of weakness, failure, poverty and death?

In the source documents of the Christian faith we discover the heartbeat of the gospel among the poor and those dismissed as failures: the poor with whom the Christ person lived, ate, drank, healed, hugged and loved.

As we look back on the gospel accounts of this person we see time and time again that it is in situations of weakness, failure and poverty that this reality is unexpectedly discovered. We see it in the heartbroken Jairus and his failure to protect his daughter from death; in the woman with the haemorrhage damned by religion and the failure of her own body.

We see it in the failure of the prodigal son to honour his father and his mother; in the outcast Samaritan who had failed to worship God in the way that others thought right; and in the sinner in the Temple repenting of his many failures and deliberate sins.

But is the Christ person we seek today, the one whom with a certain irony the Church calls its great high priest, not that self-same person? Might it not be that the heartbeat of the Gospel, the living touch of reality, is revealed to us from among the weak, the vulnerable and the failures of today's world?

Those who are not able to live a life we call normal: the homeless and the confused; the alcoholic who fails to kick the addiction; the child with cancer whose body fails it in its fight for life; the Down's syndrome girl whose mind fails to work in ways we think appropriate; the divorced priest whose failed marriage ruins his career and brings him closer to God?

Are these so different from the rag-bag bunch of slaves who failed to defend themselves from foreign aggression in Egypt and who were led out to life in the Exodus event? So different from the unrepentant thief condemned as a total failure by the most highly developed legal system in the world? And from the Christ person who failed to convince the world and now hangs next to him, dying on a cross?

In a world convinced that life is to be encountered in wealth, possessions, power, assertiveness and success; we are led stumbling and uncertain to make the ridiculous assertion that reality is to be discovered elsewhere: in an encounter and a relationship with God.

And we are led to say that that encounter is to be entered into not through our achievements but through our own vulnerability: not at those triumphant times in our life when we are lifted up by success, but when we are crushed by failure and despair.

In a world which worships success, it may be that the key to life lies in our own poverty and failure – and our willingness to listen for that reality among those dismissed as life's casualties and failures: those we call the poor.

But to see the poor as part of our own liberation and our own search for meaning and purpose is to invert the value system of the world; and to begin to see why the Christ person was so hated by the powerful.

They could not then, and cannot now, accept that reality is an event which happens. It is not a unit of wealth to be won, achieved, bought, possessed and then stored away. Reality is a gift given to anyone poor enough to have hands empty enough to receive it. But to receive it we may first need to empty our hands.

It may be the ones we reject as the worthless in our own world: dying on our TV screens, degraded in our dole queues, begging and busking on the streets of our own towns and cities who are a crucial link with this reality.

As we have seen time and time again in our journey it was the outcast and rejected Christ, who the Church calls its great high priest, who did indeed mediate the gift of life to those among whom he lived: the despised and the poor.

It was this same priest figure who tells us that when we show love for the poor, we show love for him; that he is there among them. And if then, why not now, if he is the one who is the same yesterday, today and for ever?

In our searching for reality and for meaning it may be that we discover that this gift, this precious sacrament of life, is offered to us by God. But that, like the fried egg sandwich in the park, we will receive it from the unwashed hands of the priesthood of the poor.